D1606921

WITHDRAWN

Our Family Archive

Our Family Archive

DAVID CLARK • ADAM JUNIPER

Reader's
Digest

The Reader's Digest Association, Inc.
Pleasantville, New York/Montreal/London/Sydney/Singapore

A Reader's Digest Book

This edition published by The Reader's Digest Association, Inc.,
by arrangement with Ilex Press Limited.

Copyright © 2009 The Ilex Press Limited

This book was conceived, designed, and produced by:
The Ilex Press, 210 High Street, Lewes, BN7 2NS, UK

All rights reserved. Unauthorized reproduction,
in any manner, is prohibited.

Reader's Digest is a registered trademark of
The Reader's Digest Association, Inc.

FOR ILEX PRESS
Publisher: Alastair Campbell
Creative Director: Peter Bridgewater
Managing Editor: Chris Gatcum
Art Director: Julie Weir
Designer: Ginny Zeal
Art Editor: Emily Harbison

FOR READER'S DIGEST
U.S. Project Editor: Kim Casey
Copy Editor: Marilyn Knowlton
Canadian Project Editor: Pamela Johnson
Australian Editor: Annette Carter
Project Designer: Jennifer Tokarski
Senior Art Director: George McKeon
Executive Editor, Trade Publishing: Dolores York
Associate Publisher: Rosanne McManus
President and Publisher, Trade Publishing: Harold Clarke

LIBRARY OF CONGRESS CATALOGING-IN-PUBLICATION DATA
Clark, David.
 Our family archive : super-simple tools to create a digital
family scrapbook / David Clark, Adam, Juniper.
     p. cm.
 ISBN 978-0-7621-0994-4
 1. Photographs--Conservation and restoration--Data processing.
 2. Scrapbooking--Data processing. 3. Photography--Digital techniques.
 4. Photograph albums--Data processing. 5. Digital preservation.
 I. Juniper, Adam. II. Title.
 TR465.C56 2009
 745.593--dc22
                        2008050956

We are committed to both the quality of our products and
the service we provide to our customers. We value your
comments, so please feel free to contact us.

The Reader's Digest Association, Inc.
Adult Trade Publishing
Reader's Digest Road
Pleasantville, NY 10570-7000

For more Reader's Digest products and information,
visit our website:
        www.rd.com (in the United States)
        www.readersdigest.ca (in Canada)
        www.readersdigest.co.uk (in the UK)
        www.readersdigest.com.au (in Australia)
        www.readersdigest.com.nz (in New Zealand)
        www.rdasia.com (in Asia)

Printed in and bound in China
1 3 5 7 9 10 8 6 4 2

St. Marys Public Library

31006002870434
NON FIC 025.84 C
Clark, David.
Our family archive :

Contents

Introduction

"In every conceivable manner our family is the link to our past, the bridge to our future."
—Alex Haley, the author of Roots

Families are a central part of our lives. They give us a sense of our roots, of who we are, and where we have come from. In our blood relatives we see the common threads that bind us together, so it's surprising how many of us don't have an organized archive of information about our families. In these times of rapid change, our lives are very different from those of our parents and grandparents. It follows that our children's lives will be very different from our own. Without an archive many details of a family's history can be forgotten or lost.

Our Family Archive is a way of digitally recording and storing vital information about your family's past and present in one attractive and easy-to-access database. You can use it to store relatives' names, significant dates in their lives, and special memories about them. You can also include photographs and images of other important family documents.

How you use the program is up to you, and it can take up as little or as much time as you like. You might simply want to include information from one or two generations back. However, you may find that looking into your family history can be a fascinating and absorbing hobby in itself. It may inspire you to delve far back into history and discover your own distant genealogical roots.

This book aims to get you started on that journey. It tells you how to begin gathering information and where to find it. It shows you how to input written information, how to scan and give new life to old photographs, and how to take new portraits to add to your archive. Finally, it gives you the opportunity to share the results of your work by putting your family history online.

If you decide to dig deeper into your family's past, be prepared to invest some time in your research. A great deal of information is available on the Internet, but sometimes your search may take you to new, perhaps far distant places with old family connections. In finding out about your ancestors, you may reconnect with relatives that you rarely see or meet others for the first time, further strengthening the family bond.

You may find that compiling a family archive is not just an intriguing examination of your own roots; it is also a gateway to understanding more about how people used to live. In many ways the past is not lost; it's simply waiting to be rediscovered. The results that you record in *Our Family Archive* can be passed on down through the generations for your children and grandchildren to expand on and enjoy.

So why not get started on your own family archive today? No matter how far you want to travel, the journey will be fascinating.

How It Works

The *Our Family Archive* program combines the best elements of traditional family research with the advantages of modern computing, functioning in effect like a digital scrapbook. It helps you arrange stories and information about your relatives in a way that's attractive to browse, and lets you organize your research into a single, expandable location on your computer.

Just like a real scrapbook, *Our Family Archive* stores all the details you add automatically and immediately into a file on your computer, without the need to remember to choose a "save" option. As soon as you type something, it is preserved, together with all the other names, dates, and photos you have already added to your archive.

Automatic saving isn't the only advantage of the digital scrapbook either; you can also import and replace digital pictures, add to stories, and make changes as you explore your family history further, without tearing pages out of an album or running out of space. You can even change the color scheme.

Scissors, glue, and paper
Creating a scrapbook of your family history used to be a difficult and time-consuming task, and after all that effort you would end up with only one copy.

BROWSE THE ARCHIVE ▶
VIEW THE FAMILY LIST ▶
CREATE AN ARCHIVE ▶

Our Family Archive

Using OUR FAMILY ARCHIVE you can store documents, photos and the recollections of family members and then print them out using beautifully designed, preformatted templates or you can play them as a slide show presentation. OUR FAMILY ARCHIVE puts you in charge of the project. Simply select from a wide range of template themes like Home and Garden, Sports, Military, Arts and Crafts, Work, etc., choose the text and images that you want to use and leave the rest to us.

Our Family Archive
Working on a computer helps you organize your workflow and presents you with a clean, easy-to-use interface without any messy glue or scissors.

In addition to reworking your pages when you get new information, there is also the option to print out the pages and share them with your relatives around the globe.

Finally, because *Our Family Archive* is a database that will grow according to your needs, the information is automatically sorted in the most efficient way, without your ever needing to worry about it. So no matter how many relatives you add to your archive, you'll always be able to find a particular individual quickly and easily.

You Will Need

Our Family Archive requires a relatively modest computer setup, although it is possible to take advantage of any peripherals you might have bought, such as a printer and a scanner. To get started, however, all you will need is an Apple Macintosh computer or a Microsoft Windows PC that meets the minimum system requirements below.

Another thing you will find very useful, but not essential, is access to the Internet. While *Our Family Archive* works without requiring you to log on, the *Help* tool supplied with the program links to an online resources page that will be kept current with the latest developments and any necessary updates.

Minimum Requirements: Windows PC

- Microsoft Windows XP or Vista

- Processor (CPU): 1 GHz or faster

- Memory (RAM): 256 MB (0.25 GB) or more

- Hard drive space: 200 MB minimum (more if you add a large number of pictures)

- CD-ROM drive

Minimum Requirements: Mac OS X

- Mac OS X 10.4 or 10.5

- Processor (CPU): 1 GHz or faster

- Memory (RAM): 256 MB (0.25 GB) or more

- Hard drive space: 200 MB minimum (more if you add a large number of pictures)

- CD-ROM drive (for MacBook Air, access to a CD-ROM drive on another computer)

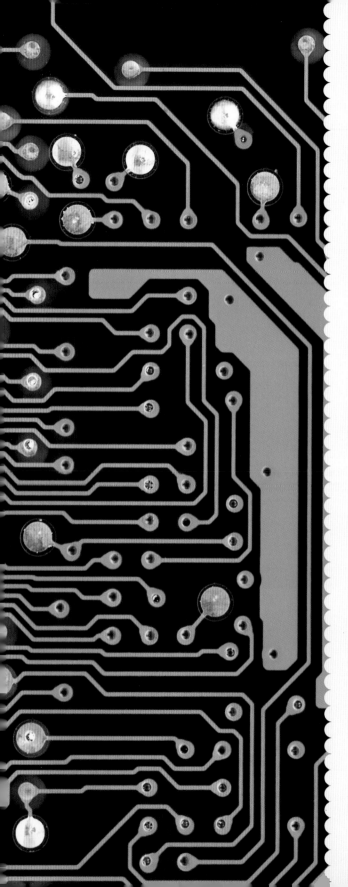

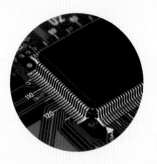

Computer Terminology

Central Processing Unit (CPU) The chip at the heart of the computer—its brain, if you like—which is behind everything else that happens. The speed needed to run *Our Family Archive* is modest by modern standards.

Random Access Memory (RAM) This is the space the computer uses to store information about to be processed by the CPU or things it will need frequently. The more you have, the faster your computer will operate. This is usually one of the cheapest components to upgrade in any computer system, and the most cost-effective. It is also relatively easy to do; even elegantly designed laptops usually allow access to the RAM for upgrades.

Screen Resolution This is a measure of the amount of information your monitor can display. Larger monitors can usually accommodate more information. However, some monitors feature smaller pixels, so they can cram more detail in the same physical space. That's why a measurement of pixels, rather than inches or centimeters, is used. For *Our Family Archive*, a minimum screen resolution of 1024 x 800 pixels is recommended.

Family Research

To compile your family archive, information is key. You'll need to assemble the important facts and figures of your relatives' and ancestors' lives, as well as the memories and family stories that help bring those facts and figures alive.

You'll also need to gather images: family group photos and individual portraits, plus other pictures that tell you something about a person's life and character. All this information, written and visual, ultimately will come together in your archive to form a unique family history.

The data that go into this archive will come from a wide range of sources. You'll find material at home, with your relatives, in official archives, and in online databases.

This chapter guides you through the first steps in researching your family history. It tells you which essential pieces of information you'll need—and where and how to find them.

Getting Organized

While compiling your archive, you will gather a lot of information and images that relate to different members of your family. As the material accumulates, it becomes easier to misplace or lose track of items. That's why it's so important for you to be organized from the beginning, whether you are starting a small family archive or embarking on research that goes back many generations.

Your information may come from family documents you find around the house or from other family members, archives and libraries, or on the Internet, so it must be portable and easy to access. Use whatever filing method suits you, but make sure it's clear and accurate for when you transfer your data to the *Our Family Archive* program. Taking a little time to get your project well organized at the start will save you a lot of time in the long run.

What You'll Need

The basic stationery items you'll need to start with are simple and inexpensive. Start with a three-ring binder and tab dividers, a pad of paper, and pens or pencils. It's a good idea to allow one sheet of paper per person at first, then add extra sheets as you find out more about the individual. Keep your notes in alphabetical order, filed under the surname first, then the given name (for example: Jones, Anna).

You can use clear plastic sleeves for storing copies of documents, such as birth, death, and marriage certificates; wills; diplomas and other certificates of achievement; family photographs and other items. If an item relating to an individual is too big to store in your binder, keep a record of where it is stored in that person's section of your notes.

As you conduct your research, you may want to acquire more information-gathering tools, such as:

- **Tape recorder** for recording interviews

- **Digital camera** for photographing relatives or items of memorabilia

- **Flatbed scanner** for copying documents or photographs and turning them into digital files.

Keeping Accurate Records

Make sure your records are as accurate as possible. If you misspell a name or incorrectly record a date of birth, the error may cause you to waste time later on, when you're searching archives, or even keep you from finding the information you're looking for.

It's a good idea to note the exact source of particular pieces of information because some sources are more reliable than others. For instance, a relative may tell you that your grandmother was born in one city, but her birth certificate may indicate that she actually was born in another city. You may have to revise details in your records if information from a more reliable source becomes available.

Where to Start

It's easy to feel daunted when you start to collect information for a family archive, but the basic materials for your research are likely to be readily available. The best place to start is right at home, with information you already know or to which you have easy access. Use documents, memorabilia, and photographs that you have on hand—and of course, your own memories—to get the ball rolling.

First, write down your own full name and the names of your immediate family members—your children, your spouse, brothers and sisters, parents, and grandparents, whether living or deceased. Add the names of any people related to them by blood or marriage, such as your siblings' spouses and children and your parents' and grandparents' siblings and as many of their descendants as possible.

The next step is to record the dates and places of each family member's birth and, if applicable, marriage and death. Check these dates against any family records you have around the house, such as birth, death, and marriage certificates. If there are gaps in your information, leave them for now; and if you don't know a date or location for certain, make it clear in your notes that it is an educated guess.

Photographs

Names, dates, and places will be important to your archive, but you'll also need to flesh out this basic information. Look through your family photograph collection for good, clear images of each family member on your list. Don't worry if the photos are damaged—there will be suggestions for ways to restore and enhance them later in this book.

Adding "Color" to Your Archive

Our Family Archive lets you record stories and anecdotes about your relatives under various headings. Try to find information that will add color to names and dates by shedding light on a person's character and interests and on the events that shaped his or her life.

These details can come from a variety of sources. Family Bibles; autograph and address books; newspaper clippings, diaries, and letters; holiday cards; scrapbooks; school or work certificates or diplomas; clothing; jewelry; travel documents; yearbooks; cookbooks; and legal papers, such as wills and deeds, may all yield fascinating details that will help bring your archive to life.

Combing through family documents and records is a good place to start, but eventually, you will have to expand your research beyond your home and involve your relatives in the project.

Family Networking

Your home can be a treasure trove of information about your family's history, but once you've exhausted that source (or even before then), it's time to start networking with other family members. They can help fill in the gaps in your own knowledge and add information, stories, and memorabilia of their own to your family archive. The more information you can get from family members, the less time you'll have to spend searching for it on the Internet or in other archives.

Involving relatives in your research can also be a great way to maintain or reestablish contact with family members you rarely see. As an added bonus, you may find that a relative also has done some family research that you can add to yours.

Approaching Relatives

Contact as many family members as possible, along with any close family friends who might be able to help. As with your own initial research, start by collecting or confirming names and significant dates and locations before asking for more detailed information about a person's character and life story.

If you're particularly interested in obtaining information on previous generations, approach the elder members of your family first. They can shed light on relatives of their own and their parents' generations, and their memories may go back a generation or more beyond that. Contact them initially by letter, phone, or e-mail. If possible, arrange a visit to talk with them in person, though you should use whatever means of communication they prefer.

Tips://dealing with relatives

- Your relatives may be able to provide family photographs, letters, and other memorabilia previously unknown to you. If you borrow pictures to scan or other items to photograph, be sure to return them promptly and in the condition you received them.

- Don't overstay your welcome. If you're establishing contact with a family member you haven't met before, keep your first visits reasonably brief. Going back for additional discussions will give your relative time to think things over and perhaps remember even more. Consider leaving behind a list of questions for your relative to review before your next meeting.

- Give something in return. Don't just treat relatives as sources of information—stay in touch with them and, if they're interested, keep them updated on the progress of your research.

What to Take with You

- Information you have already gathered.

- Items of memorabilia, such as photographs, diaries, and scrapbooks. They can provide a window on the past and prompt your relative's memories.

- A notebook, pen, and/or a tape recorder. However, you should always ask permission before taking notes or making a recording.

If you want to conduct a thorough oral history interview, see the next page for instructions on how to go about it.

Oral Histories

A great way to preserve your family's story and obtain information for your archive is to conduct a full-fledged oral history interview with one or more of your relatives. Oral histories are records of memories that would otherwise be lost to the passage of time, and historians have been using them increasingly in recent decades. To get the most out of an oral history interview, you need to be organized and prepare yourself in advance. As discussed on the previous pages, it's important to conduct the interview with tact and sensitivity.

Before the Interview

Start preparing as soon as your relative agrees to be interviewed and you pick a date that's convenient to you both. Make a list of the questions (or at least the general types of questions) you want to ask. These will differ from family to family, but there are certain main areas you should be sure to cover (see page 21).

You can record what your relative says using a paper and pen, but you'll be more likely to catch all the details if you make notes and also use a tape recorder. Well before the interview, make sure that the tape recorder is functioning—it would be very frustrating to start the interview and find out that the recorder doesn't work. You also need to get your relative's permission in advance to take notes and/or record the conversation.

Interview Procedure

- First, record the date of the interview and the interviewee's full name and date and place of birth.

- Have questions prepared, but let your relative wander off the subject if he or she wishes to—that way, you may get useful information you hadn't expected. However, guide him back to the question if he wanders too far.

- When you're talking to an elder family member about the past, tread carefully. You may unwittingly touch on a sensitive topic that he finds upsetting to talk about. If he is reluctant to discuss an issue, respect his wishes and move on.

- Don't tire your relative with a long interview—an hour at a time is long enough, especially if the person is elderly. Make the process enjoyable and interesting and not a chore!

Topics to Cover

- Ask what your relative remembers from his or her childhood. Find out where he lived, what he liked doing at various ages, and what he recalls of his school days.

- What does he remember about his own parents, siblings, and any other family members with whom he had contact?

- Does he have any information on, or stories about, his grandparents?

- Ask about his home life and family traditions. How did his family celebrate birthdays and national and religious holidays?

- What does he remember about life during wartime or other historically interesting periods?

- What was his first job, what did it involve, and how much was he paid? What other jobs has he done?

- Did he attend church or synagogue regularly? Was religion an important part of his life when he was young?

- Does he have any family items handed down through the generations?

- Ask about other topics that are relevant to your interviewee—such as hobbies, sports, musical accomplishments, military service, and so on. All could provide useful material for your archive.

Photographs

Photographs are going to be an important element of your family archive. Seeing an image of a relative really makes the dry facts and figures in your archive come alive for the reader. Also, when you preserve an image digitally, by either scanning it or rephotographing the original picture with a digital camera, you are protecting it from the ravages of time.

You can store a maximum of six images for each individual in the *Our Family Archive* program. This enables you to show a relative at different ages or doing things that say something about his or her own particular character and interests. If you don't have many pictures of an individual, perhaps a distant relative from a few generations back, you could photograph their tombstone, house, or a piece of personal memorabilia.

Identifying Who and What Is Shown

If you're using an old photograph and there's no name on the back, try to verify with more than one relative that the person in the picture is who you think it is. People can change greatly over a lifetime, and siblings can look very much like one another. If you wrongly identify your relatives, your archive will become more fiction than fact!

Dating Photographs

If there's no date on the photograph, try to establish roughly when it was taken using clues in the picture. If you know a person's date of birth, you can guess when the picture was taken by assessing his age in the photograph. You also can establish rough dates by looking carefully at the way people are dressed.

Note any information written on the back of the photo. If the picture is in its original frame, it's worth taking the photo out (carefully!) to look inside. You may find names, dates, or other information. Old newspaper may have been used as filler in the frame; if you're lucky, there might be a date on the paper. If the photograph was taken by a professional, try to find out when the photographer was in business, perhaps by looking in an old city directory.

Entire books have been written on the subject of how to date photographs by deciphering such clues as the way the subjects are dressed or the photographic techniques used. To learn more, you can go to your local library or bookstore or do some research online. Just enter "dating old photographs" in your preferred Internet search engine.

Labeling Your Photographs

It's important to label all photographs in your collection, but especially those that are going into your archive. This applies as much to new photographs that you take for the archive (such as portraits of relatives, copies of documents, or family reunion pictures) as it does to old family photographs you already have.

When you have established who's who in an old picture, the order in which they are shown, and a rough date and location, write this information on the back of the photograph. This will be useful when you scan and input the image into the *Our Family Archive* program. Be careful not to damage the photograph when you're jotting down information on the back (take extra care with old photographs). Use a pencil or a photo-labeling pen. Don't use a ballpoint pen, because the ink can show through on the front of the photograph (or even smudge onto other surfaces or photographs) and is difficult to remove.

The Passage of Time

Personal photograph albums are a good way of following a relative's life from their earliest years to the present day.

Birth, Marriage, and Death Records

Birth, marriage, and death records are known as "vital records," and the information they contain is important to anyone researching his or her family history. Vital records, completed soon after an event has taken place, are generally reliable sources of information. They take you beyond the imperfect world of people's memories and open a door to the past. For example, your grandmother's birth certificate enables you to find out more not only about her but also about your great-grandparents as well. This may, in turn help you to add more generations to your family archive.

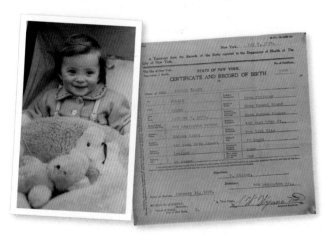

Birth Records

The exact details contained in birth certificates vary depending on when they were issued and in which locality. Nevertheless, even early birth certificates usually include the following information:

- the child's full name

- the full names of the parents

- the date and place of birth

- the child's sex and, in some cases, race.

Bear in mind that until relatively recently, many births went unrecorded, especially in rural areas.

Marriage Records

You usually can find marriage records in the civil division—county, city, town, or village—in which the wedding took place. Besides offering proof that a couple actually married, marriage records can yield valuable additional information for the family-history researcher.

There are three different types of marriage records:

- **A marriage license**—an authorization to marry issued prior to the ceremony by a local official, such as a town clerk. Note that licenses don't offer actual proof of marriage, because couples could have a license but decide not to marry.

- **The marriage register**—a full written record of all marriages in an area.

- **A marriage certificate**—an official, and sometimes elaborate, document completed by the official at the wedding.

These records list the full names of the bride and groom prior to the marriage and, in the case of marriage registers and certificates, the date and location of the wedding. They also may include other information, such as:

- the bride and groom's age and date of birth

- their occupation and place of residence

- their marital status prior to the wedding (single, widowed or divorced, and notes of any previous marriages).

Death Records

It's often easier to find death records than birth or marriage records, mainly because they are the most recent records on an individual. At the very least death records provide the name of the deceased and the date and place of death. They also can sometimes tell you:

- the person's age at death

- time and cause of death

- marital status, place of residence, and occupation

- date and place of birth

- names of the deceased's parents

- place of burial.

However, it's worth remembering that the information on a death record is usually provided by a (possibly distraught) relative or friend and may not be complete or wholly accurate.

How to Find Vital Records

To find vital records (or vital statistics as they are often called in Commonwealth countries), contact the Office (or Registry) of Vital Records of the locality in which the birth, marriage, or death that you're researching took place.

Alternatively, a number of websites provide details on how to obtain the records you want. A good place to start is *www.genealogy.about.com*, which provides information on finding records in a wide range of countries, including the U.S, U.K, Canada, Australia, and New Zealand.

Census Records

Census records preserve snapshots of your relatives and ancestors as they were on particular days in history. They can supplement information given in birth, death, and marriage records and provide fascinating insights into family life. They also can reveal otherwise hard-to-trace details about family members and provide a springboard to additional research.

Over the course of the 18th and 19th centuries, the practice of conducting a systematic national census at set intervals became increasingly widespread. The U.S. Federal Population Census began in 1790, while the United Kingdom conducted its first modern census in 1801.

In many countries—including the U.S. and the U.K.—censuses are held every 10 years, but some nations, like Canada, Australia, and New Zealand, conduct censuses at five-year intervals. Because the personal information in census records is confidential it is usually processed and published in a way that makes it impossible to identify individuals. Some countries, including Australia (after 1901) destroy

the actual records after processing; others subject them to a lengthy embargo. The embargo period in the U.S., for example, is 72 years, but it's 100 years in the U.K. Thus, the most recent records available to the public in the U.S. are those from the 1930 census and from the 1901 censuses in the U.K and Canada.

What's in Census Records

Early census records offer limited information, but from the 1850s onward, census records developed enormously to include much more data. The exact information collected varies from country to country and from one census to the next, but census records usually contain some or all of the following facts:

- names of family members
- full street address
- family members' ages at a certain point in time
- state or country of birth
- birthplaces of parents
- year of immigration
- marital status
- occupation(s)
- whether they have done military service
- the value of their home and personal belongings

How to Access Census Records

Finding census records has become much easier with the advent of the Internet, but you can still examine microfilmed archive material if you wish. Either way, you need to know the full name of a relative or ancestor and the locality in which he or she resided at the time of the census. Here are some of the ways you can access census records:

• Internet sites, including *www.ancestry.com*, *www.ancestry.com.au*, *www.ancestry.ca*, *www.ancestry.co.uk*, *www.censusfinder.com*, *www.genealogy.com,*and *www.heritagequestonline.com*, hold a large number of census records. These subscription sites usually charge fees for accessing information, but may be available free at certain libraries (check locally). Free access to international data is also available at *www.familysearch.org* while U.S. data is available at *www.us-census.org*.

• The usual repository for a country's census records is its National Archives, but state, provincial, and other local archives and record offices may also hold microfilm or microfiche copies of census records from their areas.

Neither the U.S. National Archives (*www.archives.gov/genealogy/census/*) nor the Library and Archives Canada (*www.collectionscanada.gc.ca/genealogy*) post census records on their websites.

• In the U.S., microfilmed records can be consulted on site at no charge at the National Archives building in Washington, D.C. and at regional National Archives facilities throughout the country. (In addition, subscription online services, such as *ancestry.com* or *heritagequest.com*, are available free-of-charge at National Archives facilities.)

• In Canada, census records can be viewed at Library and Archives Canada in Ottawa or at regional libraries. The British National Archives (*www.nationalarchives.gov.uk/census*) makes census records available both online and on site. You also can research international census records at the Family History Library in Salt Lake City, Utah, or at one of its local Family History Centers (see *www.familysearch.org*).

Immigration and Emigration

Immigration has shaped the history and population of many countries, especially those of the New World, such as the United States, Canada, Australia, and New Zealand. But even in the Old World, Britain and Western Europe have become magnets for immigrants from former colonies in African and Asia, for workers from within and without the European Union, and for asylum-seekers from the around the globe.

People emigrate from one country to another for many reasons—to escape poverty and hardship, to avoid political or religious persecution, or simply to find a new life in a prosperous and progressive nation. Whatever may have impelled your ancestors to leave home, discovering more about their country (or countries) of origin can be a crucial part of your family history research.

Tracing Your Family Overseas

To trace ancestors from overseas, you will need to know, or find out:

- The original version of the person's full name. Some immigrants changed their names upon arrival in their new homeland to fit in better and feel less foreign. In some cases new arrivals had their names changed by immigration officials.

- Your ancestor's birthplace. You need this information because most overseas records are held at the local, not national, level.

- The name of a relative with known ties to your ancestor, in order to distinguish the ancestor in question from someone else who has the same name.

- Your ancestor's birth date, marriage date (if married abroad), or the date of another significant event in his life.

Where you'll find this information depends on when and from where your ancestors emigrated and on other factors, such as their religious affiliation and ethnicity. Good sources to start with include vital records; census, military, and church records; family letters; school or work certificates; and other personal memorabilia. National immigration records are another excellent source of information.

Immigration Records

A nation's immigration records (usually ship-passenger arrival records) provide family-history researchers with a range of details about arrivals in that country from foreign ports. This information may include:

- nationality and place of birth

- age, height, and color of hair

- town or city of last residence

- occupation

- the name of the ship on which the new immigrant traveled and date of entry to the new land.

How to Find Immigration Records

The easiest way to find and study immigration records is via the Internet. Try searching the following sites:

• **National archives websites**
  The National Archives of countries such as the United States, Canada, and Great Britain hold extensive collections of passenger lists and other immigration records, and their websites (see page 27) provide instructions for accessing them. The National Archives of Australia (*www. naa.gov.au*) has embarked on a project to make nearly all of the nation's immigration records available online.

• ***www.castlegarden.org* and *www.ellisisland.org***
  Castle Garden, today known as Castle Clinton National Monument, was the first official U.S. immigration center. This site has information on some 10 million immigrants to the United States between 1830 and 1892. The Ellis Island Immigration Station opened in New York Harbor in 1892. Its website contains records of more than 20 million immigrants who arrived in New York from 1892 to 1924.

• ***www.pier21.ca***
  Pier 21, Canada's Immigration Museum, houses a growing collection of stories, oral histories, documents, and images covering immigration to Canada. Its website contains a number of links, details about the museum's research services, and a ship arrival database dating back to 1928, amongst other useful items.

Delving Deeper

In the first chapter you learned the first steps in researching your family history and assembling the important facts about your relatives' and ancestors' lives. For some that might be enough. Perhaps you've achieved your objective and discovered all you wanted to know about your family.

But if you want to delve deeper and create a more detailed portrait of the lives of your family members, read on. In this chapter you will discover sources of information that will help you understand your family in more detail. Records of education, occupation, military service, and church activity can tell you a great deal about your forebears. You will also look at the significant information available in legal documents, such as wills and land records, and find additional ways to continue expanding and enriching your family archive.

Education

Some people do not enjoy school, others love it; but there's no doubt that the time we spend at school is a crucial, formative period in our lives. It's a time for learning, growing, and making friendships, and the things we learn at school and the people we meet there can influence our whole lives.

Some of the younger relatives included in your archive may still be at school or have recently left, so their school experiences will be central to their lives. However, do not overlook report cards, photographs, and achievement prizes of older relatives and ancestors. Attendance records, sometimes published and filed in libraries and archives, can yield valuable family history information, as can school yearbooks.

School Report Cards

Report cards often provide valuable insights into a child's development and tell you something about the direction a person's life is likely to take. If you're talking to older relatives about their lives, ask them what they remember about their school days. If they're comfortable talking about the subject, ask whether they have any school report cards they might be willing to show you. These documents may spark additional memories, and teachers' remarks can be insightful—and, with the benefit of hindsight, sometimes amusing.

School report cards of previous generations of your family can also be fascinating, so look for them among family memorabilia. If you come across a particularly interesting report card, you may want to scan or photograph it so that you can include it in your archive.

Achievement Prizes and Certificates

Prizes and certificates demonstrate abilities in a particular field and are often cherished mementoes for individuals and their loved ones. A prize for sports achievement or for a musical or other artistic talent may foreshadow a lifelong involvement in that field.

School Yearbooks

School and college yearbooks, some of them dating back to the early 1900s, are often rich repositories of information. Student and faculty lists, photographs of student groups, and summaries of the year's academic and sports achievements and major social events all provide unique glimpses into an age, as well as useful material on individuals.

If you don't have access to a forebear's yearbooks but know where and when he or she went to school, it would be worth seeking out the school's yearbooks for that period. They might reveal something unexpected about the person, such as a school prize or the captainship of a school team that he may have been too modest to brag about.

Where to Find Yearbooks

School yearbooks can be found in the school's local community library, and they are often sold in secondhand bookshops or on eBay. Some have been scanned and can be viewed on websites such as *www.old-yearbooks.com* and *www.ancestry. com*, or on the school's site. Another website, *www.genealogy.about.com/cs/yearbooks*, provides links to online yearbook collections.

Ancestry.com's "Community" pages often include messages from people trying to find school yearbooks or from those who own yearbooks and are willing to look up information.

Occupations

As with some of the other family history research sources discussed in this chapter, occupational records are not among the most obvious. Also, an individual's work records are not always easy to access, but when they are available, they can be very rewarding to the family historian. Occupational records can confirm and expand on information you already have and sometimes they add considerably to your knowledge of a relative's or ancestor's life.

Hidden away in archives in your country are records on employees, trade and professional licenses, and union memberships. Many trade associations and individual companies keep information on their members and employees, and their directories, almanacs, and company histories can cast light on an ancestor's work life. If a company is no longer in business, its records may have been deposited in a library or archive.

Finding Out More about Occupations

For most of us, work is central to our lives. When you're compiling your archive, ask your living relatives about their occupations—how they got into that profession or trade, what they like about it, and any special things they have achieved during the course of their work.

You can find out about an ancestor's occupation from several possible sources:

- **Census records** from the mid-19th century onward (in earlier censuses information on each household member's occupation may have been scant or nonexistent).

- **Legal records,** such as wills, military, and pension records.

- **Vital records,** including marriage and death certificates.

- **City directories,** which list not only the names and occupations of the local residents but also local businesses.

To locate the appropriate occupational records, you need to find out:

- an individual's exact occupation

- dates of employment in this work

- exact company names, where applicable.

Availability of Records

The existence and availability of occupational records will depend on your ancestor's job and the country and period in which he or she lived. For example, you may have found out from census records that your great-grandfather worked for the U.S. government. In that case you are in luck because federal employee records can be found in the Official Register of the United States, a publication produced by the United States Civil Service Commission. Records date back to the mid-19th century. In other countries, the National Archives and/or Library may hold records relating to government employees. In general, however, historical employment records may be difficult or even impossible to find, although you may be able to discover details about an ancestor's place of work or the kind of work he or she did.

Other Sources

There are many websites that can help you in your search for a relative's occupational records, and an excellent starting point is *www.cyndislist.com/ occupatn.htm*, which provides links to websites relating to occupations and general resource sites, as well as information on libraries, archives, museums, and relevant societies and groups that may be able to assist you in your research.

Tip://surnames

A clue to a forebear's occupation can sometimes be found in your family surname. Butcher, Baker, and Miller are obvious examples, but some others —Zimmerman (carpenter), Fletcher (maker of bows and arrows), and Ferrari (blacksmith)—are less obvious. Check dictionaries of surname meanings for clues to family occupations in previous generations.

Military Service Records

It's almost a certainty that many of your relatives and ancestors will have served in the military at some time in their lives. In some cases, military service—perhaps during wartime—may have been the major formative experience of a relative's life. If you have living relatives who have served their country, ask them about their military experiences and any memorabilia they may have kept. You can find out about forebears who saw military service by searching official records. Military service records also can provide a surprising amount of additional information.

What Military Records Are Available?

- **Compiled Service Records** list a service member's rank, unit, and dates of joining and leaving the military. They also provide military information (such as awards and medals received) and biographical and medical data.

- **Draft Records** such as birth date, occupation, employer, and other personal data—on people who registered for military drafts.

- **Military Pension Applications and Pension Payments Records**—the application files in particular—contain a great deal of backup documentation, such as service records, birth records, marriage and death certificates (where applicable), family letters, legal papers, and other military documents.

- **Death Lists and Casualty Indexes** provide information on military personnel killed or wounded during active service.

If you have ancestors who served in the U.S. military before 1855, Bounty Land Warrant Application Files are well worth investigating. These files refer to land claims based on military service between 1775 and 1855. Canadian land petitions of the 18th and 19th centuries may also contain information about military petitioners and their families. (See also Land Records, pages 42–43.)

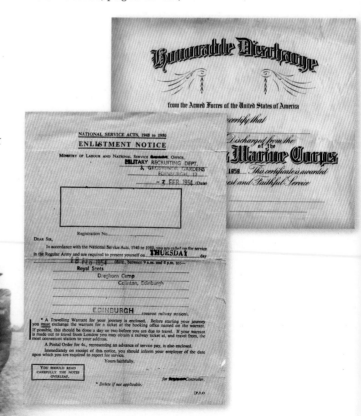

How to Access Military Records

To access the correct records, you need to know as much as possible about the person you are researching. At the very least you should know your relative's full name and any nicknames, plus the military branch in which he served and his dates of service. It will also help to know if he served in the Regular Army or in a reserve force (the U.S. National Guard, Canadian Forces Reserve, and the U.K. Territorial Army, for example) and in which conflicts he took part. The best place to start your search of military records is online.

- Websites such as the *www.ancestry.com* sites (*.com/military, .com.au, .co.uk,* and *.ca*) and *www.militaryrecordsarchive.com* contain thousands of official records and millions of individual names.

- The usual repository for a nation's military service records is its national archives. Depending on the country and the policy of the archives, military records may be viewed online and/or on-site, and access, especially to more recent records, may be restricted. See the military records section of a national archives' website (for example, *www. archives.gov* (U.S.), *www.collectionscanada. gc.ca*, *www.nationalarchives.gov.uk*, *www. naa.gov.au*, *www.archives.govt.nz*) to find out what information is available and how you can access it.

Church Records

Church records are sometimes overlooked by family historians, but they can fill in the gaps where civil records of births, marriages, and deaths are not available or supplement the information in existing civil records. However, church records can be difficult to locate. You may not know your ancestor's denomination, or the particular church he or she attended may no longer exist. Unfortunately, there is no centralized source for church records. These problems are discussed below, but first, take a look at the kinds of records that are available.

Types of Church Records

Most churches keep the following on hand:

- **Baptism/christening records** These records show the date and place of birth, as well as that of the christening or baptism. They also may include the name of the child's parents and their place of residence.

- **Marriage records** The contents of these records vary according to religion and denomination. The most basic records list only the names of the bride and groom and the date they were married. Others may include the couple's ages, place of residence, occupations, and the names of their parents.

- **Death records** A church's death register lists the name of the deceased and the date and location of the burial.

Churches may also have a number of other records, such as:

- **Membership records** These include the names of new or departing members and those who have been censured or excommunicated.

- **Minutes of meetings** These records may include mention of an ancestor's activities or opinions.

- **Obituaries** These are published in church newspapers and often contain useful and interesting information.

Finding Records

First, you need to ascertain your ancestor's religious affiliation. It may be the same as your own, or it may not. Your ancestor may even have changed religion or denomination during his or her lifetime. Such sources as obituaries, wills, death certificates, and legal papers can help shed light on your ancestor's religious life.

Once you have determined your ancestor's religious affiliation and the particular church she attended during the period you're researching, you still have to locate the church records pertaining to her. If the church she attended still exists, start your search there and continue, if necessary, at the regional or diocesan level (all the churches under the authority of a bishop) of the church in question. If a particular church has closed, its records may be stored in:

- local archives

- local history societies or libraries

- the homes of retired pastors or their families.

Many church records also have been microfilmed by the Latter-Day Saints (Mormon) Family History Library. Check the Library's pages at *www. familysearch.org*—a search of its archives can save you a lot of time and effort. Other church records can be found at *www.awesomegenealogy. com/churchrecords* and *www.rootsweb.ancestry. com/~usgenweb/churches*.

Other Faiths and Religious Groups

To research records kept by religious institutions in other faiths, start by looking at Cyndi's List of Genealogy Sites on the Internet (*www.cyndislist. com*). Simply enter the name of the particular faith or religious group, and follow the special interest links.

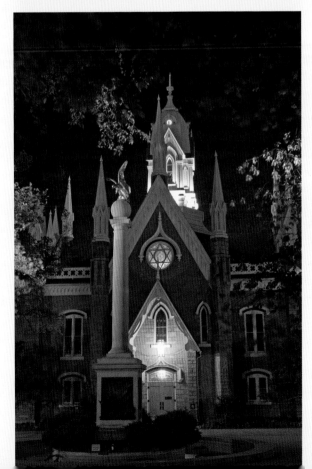

Legal Records

Legal documents, such as wills and probate and court records, are another source of useful family history information. They are used less often in family history research than vital records, census records, and immigration records. That's partly because legal documents are harder to access, and also because family historians tend to overlook them or doubt their usefulness. But as you'll see, legal records can add another dimension to your research. You may have to work a little harder to find them, but they may give you interesting additional insights into your family's history.

Wills

Wills can run to several pages or more and are likely to include information about close or distant family members who stand to inherit all or part of a person's estate. The information in a will can:

- clarify family relationships

- provide details about a person's wealth and their lifestyle

- indicate a place of burial.

Some individuals, particularly those without immediate family heirs, will have bequeathed money, property, or possessions to a number of people. This information may help embellish or fill in gaps in your family history knowledge.

Where to Find Wills

How to go about finding an ancestor's will, assuming he or she left one, depends on where and when the individual lived. Wills are usually held in the state, province, county or district in which the testator (the person who left the will) lived. They are filed in the jurisdiction's probate court or registry (see below) according to the year in which they were executed.

Probate Records

Probate is a legal process that determines the validity of a will, enforces its provisions, and oversees the equitable distribution of the property of people who die intestate (without leaving a will). Probate records include wills, lists of assets, creditors and heirs, and other documents that are often very useful in family history research. The papers contained in probate files can help you:

- document family relationships and surviving family members

- calculate the total value of an ancestor's estate, including land and property

- discover family origins in another country.

Where to Find Probate Records

Like wills, probate records are stored in local court archives or registries, usually at the provincial or county level. If you're looking for the probate records of a particular ancestor, check the probate court archives in the jurisdiction in which he or she resided. If your ancestor owned land or property in more than one jurisdiction, the records are likely to be held in the one in which most of his property was located. For more information consult the website of the probate court or registry in the relevant locality.

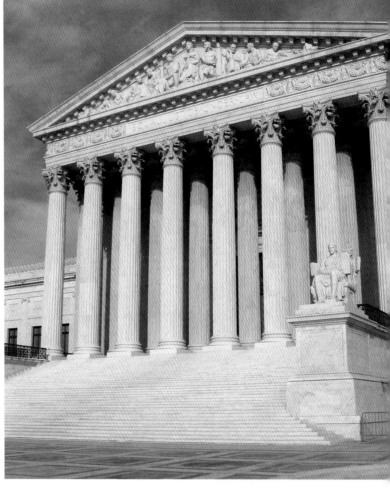

Court Records

Court records are another possible source of information for your archive. They may contain vital records and other family details, as well as information on an ancestor's employment and places of residence. Types of court cases worth investigating include divorce, partition suits and other estate disputes, and guardianship and adoption cases.

Court records, however, are not always easy to find. They are held in state, provincial, or county records offices or court archives, either on microfilm or as actual records, and in some cases, online. Websites such as *www.publicrecordcenter.com/ onlinecourtrecords.htm* (U.S.), *www.hmcourts-service.gov.uk/HMCSCourtFinder*, and *www. lawlink.nsw.gov.au* provide links to state and/or county courts; Statistics Canada publishes a National Directory of Courts in Canada, downloadable free-of-charge at its website, *www.statcan.ca.*

Land Records

Throughout history, land ownership and careful record keeping have gone hand in hand. And while land records may not sound like the most obvious source of family history information, they contain plenty of useful detail on a surprising number of people. The numbers were especially large in the New World, where the prospect of land ownership was a powerful magnet for successive waves of immigrants.

If you are tracing your family history back several generations, you may find useful information in the different types of land records that are available, such as patents, surveys, and warrants. They may help you locate other records, such as census, court, or military records, and in some cases they even turn out to be the best records available on an individual ancestor.

Land records tell us:

- where an ancestor lived and for how long

- his previous county or state of residence

- in some cases, his next place of residence

- his wife's name and, sometimes, detailed information about her

- additional family information if the land was sold to a relative.

Steps for Finding Land Records:

- **If you know the county or district** in which your ancestor lived and the approximate dates he or she lived there, begin your search at the county clerk's office or the local land registry office. Consult the grantor-grantee (seller-buyer) indexes, if available, to locate the land transactions you're looking for. In addition to naming buyers and sellers, these indexes tell you, among other things, the size, location, and date of sale of a given property. They also indicate where to find the full entry in the area's deed books.

- **Locate the original deeds** (or a copy on microfilm) from the grantor and grantee indexes. Take a copy for your records; it will prove useful when you're compiling your family archive.

Bounty Land Records

From 1788 to 1855, the U.S. government offered military bounty land warrants to soldiers as payment for military service and to encourage enlistments during conflicts including the American Revolution, the War of 1812, and the Mexican War. The land was mainly in eastern and central public land states and was often sold off promptly, though some of it was retained and passed on to the soldiers' heirs. These records are held at the National Archives Building in Washington, D.C. (some are available on microfilm), and they can yield a good deal of information about an ancestor, including:

- the individual's age and place of residence at the time he applied for the warrant and his birthplace

- his rank, military unit, place of enlistment, and length of service

- dates of marriages and deaths

- family letters.

Bounty land warrants are among the more than ten million individual land transaction records held at the U.S. National Archives (*www.archives.gov/genealogy/land*). In addition, many records for the eastern states are held by the Bureau of Land Management. This collection includes three million federal land title records for Eastern Public Land States, issued between 1820 and 1908. Details are available on *www.glorecords.blm.gov.*

National Archives Land Records

The British government also used land grants to encourage settlement and reward military service in Canada and Australia. Early settlers in Canada had to submit a petition to the Governor in order to obtain Crown lands. These land petitions and the later records of homestead land grants in Western Canada can contain valuable genealogical information. Library and Archives Canada (*www.collectionscanada.gc.ca/genealogy*), as well as provincial archives and government offices, are the main repositories of these and other historical Canadian land records. For land grants and purchases in Australia, contact State Records.

Cemeteries and Burial Places

There's no doubt that the availability of records online and on microfilm has made the process of researching family history a great deal easier. However, there's nothing quite like finding an ancestor's actual resting place, probably very close to where the person lived, to make you feel connected to the past. Burial records provide birth and death dates and other useful information that you may not be able find elsewhere, while tombstones sometimes include special family inscriptions or epitaphs that tell you something about a person's life.

How to Find an Ancestor's Burial Place

- **Unless you already know** where an ancestor is buried, you first need to locate a death certificate. That document, or perhaps an obituary, may specify the cemetery in which the burial was to take place.

- **If you can't find a mention of the cemetery,** you'll need to find out your ancestor's place of residence at the time of death—perhaps from the death certificate, census records, or a will.

- **With that information** you can then look up a list of cemeteries in that locality. A useful website is *www.cemeteryjunction.com*, which lists more than 48,000 U.S. cemeteries, 2,100 Canadian cemeteries, and nearly 500 in Australia in its online directory. You can also consult published national or regional cemetery directories.

- **Once you have located the cemetery** in which your ancestor is buried, try to find a published list of tombstone inscriptions in that cemetery. This will help you confirm that your ancestor is buried there and makes it easier to find the grave on your visit. An increasing number of transcriptions of cemetery records and tombstone inscriptions are available on websites such as *www.interment.net, www. genealogy.com, www.ancestry.com*, and others. Books of transcribed inscriptions also can be found at public libraries.

- **At the cemetery** ask the sexton or caretaker how to find the tombstone you're looking for. Once you find it, make your own careful note of the inscription, take a photograph or two, then take some time to think about your ancestor and his life.

Military Veterans

If you are searching for the burial place of a U.S. military veteran you believe is interred in a U.S. national cemetery, you can search burial records online at the Department of Veterans Affairs website, *www.cem.va.gov* (U.S.).

Alternatively the Veterans Affairs Canada's website (*www.vac-acc. gc.ca*) and the Royal Canadian Legion's website (*www.legion.ca*) can be searched for details of Canadian servicemen and women.

The Commonwealth War Graves Comission (*www.cwgc.org*) also holds records for soldiers from Canada, as well as those from Australia, India, New Zealand, South Africa, and the U.K.

Other Sources

As this chapter has shown, family history information of various kinds can be found in many places, both obvious and unexpected. These sources can help supplement information you already have from census or vital records, or supply new data that doesn't exist elsewhere. Listed below are other places where you might find information for your family archive.

Newspapers

Newspapers and periodicals are often very useful sources of family history details that are not recorded anywhere else. Your ancestors may be mentioned in:

- marriage notices
- birth announcements
- legal notices
- obituaries.

Some websites allow you to search for names in their online collections of newspapers. For example, *www.ancestry.com* offers subscription-based access to millions of pages from more than 1,000 newspaper titles from the United States, the United Kingdom, and Canada, some dating back as far as the 1700s. Another site, *www.genealogybank. com*, offers access to material published in more than 2,500 historical U.S. newspapers.

Passport Applications

Useful family history information can be found in passport applications, particularly for people born overseas. The specific information required on passport applications varies depending on where and when the application was made, but it will often include:

- date and place of birth
- physical characteristics
- occupation
- foreign destination(s).

In the United States, passport applications made from 1795 to 1925 are held by the National Archives and can be viewed at the National Archives Building in Washington, D.C., and at some of its regional facilities. Those made from 1925 to the present are held at the U.S. Department of State. Paper copies of these applications can be ordered by mail from the State Department. (See the Passport pages on *www. travel.state.gov.*)

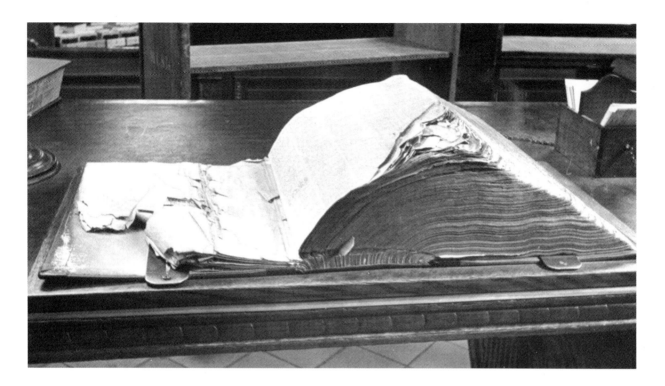

Passport records may be less complete in other countries. The Canadian Passport office, for example, does not retain expired passports or passport applications, and Library and Archives Canada holds only a few samples for historical purposes. Similarly, the National Archives of the U.K. holds only a limited number of registers and records of British passports. (The U.K. Passport Service has been keeping scanned copies of passport applications only since 2001.) In Australia, National Archives (*www.naa. gov.au*) holds some early passport records.

City Directories

City directories have been published since the 1700s. They are available in printed form and as microfilm, either in local repositories or national libraries/archives such as the U.S. Library of Congress (*www.loc.gov/rr/microform/uscity*) and Library and Archives Canada (*www. collectionscanada.gc.ca/canadiandirectories*).

They were usually published annually and include the names and occupations of residents, as well as a list of all local businesses. A useful starting point for city-directory research is the website *www. uscitydirectories.com*, which identifies repositories of U.S. directories. The contents of a large number of directories and member lists also can be found on genealogical sites, such as *www.ancestry.com*.

Other National Archives Resources

As you've seen throughout this chapter, a country's national archives is a rich repository of genealogical information. In addition to census, military, land, and court records, national archives can be useful sources for material on:

- ethnic heritage and multicultural resources

- immigration and naturalization records

- income tax and employment records

- maritime records

Continuing Your Research

You now have the information you need to start discovering your heritage and building an impressive family archive. The number of generations you record and the amount of research you do is up to you. If you have been truly bitten by the family history bug, there are many ways in which you can continue your research.

Hire a Professional Genealogist

If you hit a brick wall in your research, you might consider hiring the services of a professional genealogist. The Association of Professional Genealogists is an umbrella organization that maintains directories of researchers and their specialty areas of knowledge sorted by name, location, research field, or geographic specialty. A search on the association's website, *www.apgen. org*, will help you find the expert you need.

Additional Research

Family history research is more popular than ever before, and there are an ever-growing number of websites that deal with this absorbing subject. Typing "family history" or "genealogy" into your search engine will give you a list of sites currently available. There are dozens—if not hundreds—of books on all aspects of family history. Lists of useful books can be found on some of the websites mentioned above, or you can search for genealogy books at retail and online stores.

Join a Genealogy Society

Joining a genealogy society is a great way to meet and learn from others who share an interest in the past. There are thousands of societies around the world and one of the largest in the United States is the National Genealogical Society (*www. ngsgenealogy.org*). For lists of genealogical societies in all 50 U.S. states, Canada, Ireland, and the United Kingdom, go to the websites of the Federation of Genealogical Societies (U.S.), *www. fgs.org*, and of the Federation of Family History Societies (U.K.), *www.ffhs.org.uk*. You can also search for local genealogical societies in the United States and Canada on *www.familyhistory.com/ societyhall*, while *www.coraweb.com.au* has links to a wide number of societies across Australia.

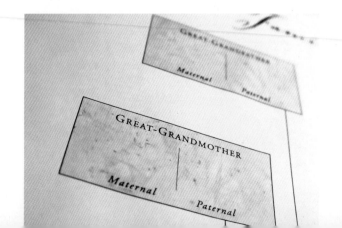

Online research
There are a lot of websites that you can use for additional research into your family history, which will help you find out more information about your ancestors.

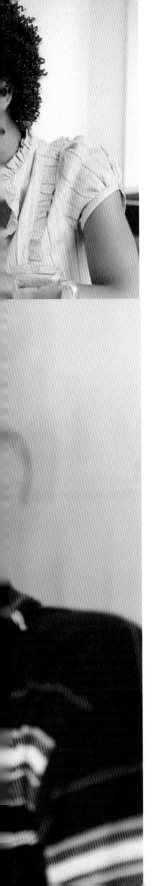

Starting the Program

Included with this book is the *Our Family Archive* program, a complete database application that allows you to enter, edit, and export details about all your relatives and ancestors. The preceding chapters explained how to find those details by researching your family's history. This chapter is all about the program itself: how to install it and how it works.

The chapter concludes with a gallery of the designs, or themes, that you can apply to your database pages. This useful reference will give you a clear idea of what your final archive pages will look like, depending on the themes you choose.

St. Marys Public Library

What Is Our Family Archive?

The program that is supplied with this book is, technically speaking, a database. If you're not used to computers, you may be unfamiliar with the term, but a database is simply a tool for storing information in an ordered way. The *Our Family Archive* database stores any information that you type in it—names, dates, facts, figures—as well as digital images you might want to include. Once information is entered in the database, you and anyone you share your family archive with will be able to access it and correct and update it, if necessary.

Database Basics

Of course, *Our Family Archive* is just one example of a digital database. Businesses use all sorts of databases for many different purposes, such as storing names and addresses of customers and other details about them or keeping track of inventory. Whatever the purpose of a database, there are certain key terms that apply to all of them:

- **Record:** Every time you add a new family member to your family archive, you are creating a new record. A record is all of the information stored in the database pertaining to a single person, item, or subject.

- **Field:** Within each record there can be more than one type of information. Each type—for example, name, date of birth, and place of birth—constitutes a field.

- **Record ID:** Because it is possible for the same information to be entered twice in more than one record—you may, for example, want to create records for two people with the same names—the computer automatically generates a unique identification number for each new record that you add.

One advantage of storing your family members' details in a database is that you can ask the computer to display it in different ways and in different sequences to help you find what you're looking for instantly.

Contacts Book
This simple form of database gives you a clear idea of how a real database works. The equivalents of fields and records are shown, but because you're writing on a printed page, there is no need for a record ID.

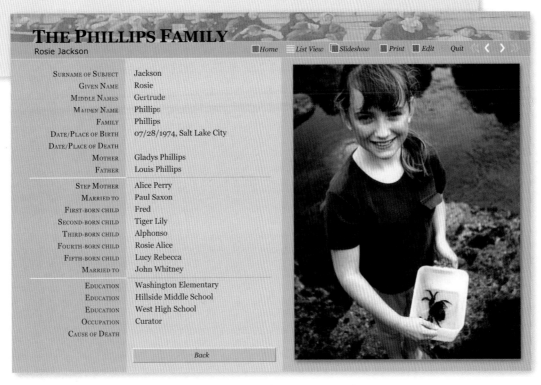

OUR FAMILY ARCHIVE

☐ *Home*   ⊞ *Add Record*   ☒ *Delete Record*   ☐ *Themes*   ☐ *Quit*   « ‹ › »

Surname	Given name	Family	Born	Mother	Father	Record ID
Davies	Graham	Davies	07/28/1884	Gladys Phillips	Louis Phillips	002
Stockbridge	Daisy	Phillips	05/04/1886	Gladys Phillips	Louis Phillips	006
Stockbridge	Daisy	Phillips	01/11/1894	Gladys Phillips	Louis Phillips	007
Stockbridge	Louis	Phillips	10/14/1902	Doris Phillips	Stanley Phillips	008
Stockbridge	Tessa	Phillips	11/30/1911	Doris Phillips	Stanley Phillips	010
Stockbridge	Rose	Phillips	04/12/1916	Doris Phillips	Stanley Phillips	011
Philips	Rose	Phillips	04/26/1938	Nancy Phillips	Nancy Phillips	012
Bailey	Bill	Phillips	08/16/1942	Nancy Phillips	Nancy Phillips	013
Phillips	Gertie	Phillips	09/01/1945	Nancy Phillips	Nancy Phillips	014
Morse	Tessa	Phillips	01/10/1947	Elizabeth Phillips	Elizabeth Phillips	015
Jackson	Heather	Phillips	11/11/1972	Elizabeth Phillips	Elizabeth Phillips	016
Jackson	Rosie	Phillips	12/25/1980	Elizabeth Phillips	Elizabeth Phillips	017

THE PHILLIPS FAMILY

Rosie Jackson

☐ *Home*   ☐ *List View*   ☐ *Slideshow*   ☐ *Print*   ☐ *Edit*   *Quit*   ‹ ›

SURNAME OF SUBJECT	Jackson
GIVEN NAME	Rosie
MIDDLE NAMES	Gertrude
MAIDEN NAME	Phillips
FAMILY	Phillips
DATE/PLACE OF BIRTH	07/28/1974, Salt Lake City
DATE/PLACE OF DEATH	
MOTHER	Gladys Phillips
FATHER	Louis Phillips
STEP MOTHER	Alice Perry
MARRIED TO	Paul Saxon
FIRST-BORN CHILD	Fred
SECOND-BORN CHILD	Tiger Lily
THIRD-BORN CHILD	Alphonso
FOURTH-BORN CHILD	Rosie Alice
FIFTH-BORN CHILD	Lucy Rebecca
MARRIED TO	John Whitney
EDUCATION	Washington Elementary
EDUCATION	Hillside Middle School
EDUCATION	West High School
OCCUPATION	Curator
CAUSE OF DEATH	

Back

Alternative Views
A database can display a record as part
of a list of records or individually.

Installing on a PC

Our Family Archive looks the same and works identically on an Apple Macintosh (Mac) or a Windows-based personal computer (PC), but how you install it differs slightly depending on your computer's operating system. The *Our Family Archive* disc contains the necessary software for both systems. This section shows you how to install the program on a Windows-based PC; to install it on a Mac, see page 56.

You cannot add information to, or otherwise change, the *Our Family Archive* database while it's stored on the CD-ROM disc. That's why it's essential that you install the program on your computer. Once you've copied the program onto your computer's hard drive, you can add all the family history information and photos you like. Installing *Our Family Archive* on a PC is simple thanks to the automatic installer program on the disc. Here's how it works:

Tip://AutoPlay problems

If you have disabled the *AutoPlay* feature on your computer, the disc will not start automatically. If that's the case, locate the CD-ROM via Windows Explorer, right-click on it, and choose *Run* from the *AutoPlay* options.

1 **Preparation** Turn on your computer and log on as you normally would. If you are already working on the computer, you don't need to close any other programs, as long as you can see the *Windows Task Bar*.

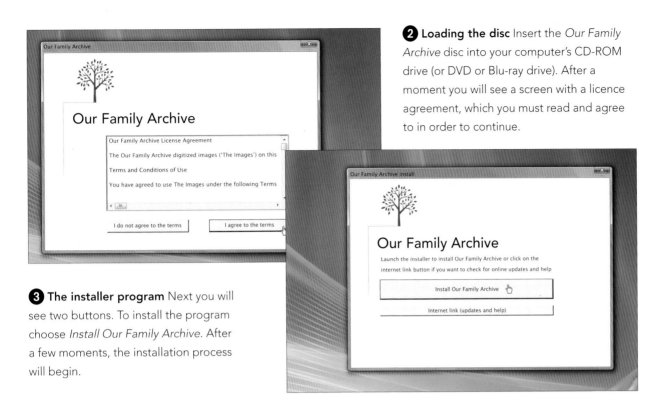

2 Loading the disc Insert the *Our Family Archive* disc into your computer's CD-ROM drive (or DVD or Blu-ray drive). After a moment you will see a screen with a licence agreement, which you must read and agree to in order to continue.

3 The installer program Next you will see two buttons. To install the program choose *Install Our Family Archive*. After a few moments, the installation process will begin.

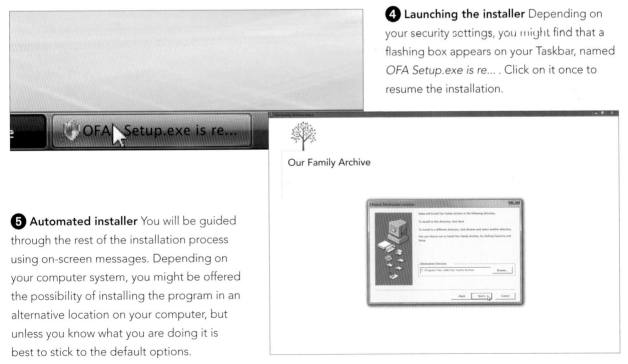

4 Launching the installer Depending on your security settings, you might find that a flashing box appears on your Taskbar, named *OFA Setup.exe is re...* . Click on it once to resume the installation.

5 Automated installer You will be guided through the rest of the installation process using on-screen messages. Depending on your computer system, you might be offered the possibility of installing the program in an alternative location on your computer, but unless you know what you are doing it is best to stick to the default options.

Installing on an Apple Macintosh

As mentioned on page 54, the *Our Family Archive* program works in the same way on a Windows-based PC or an Apple Macintosh (Mac), but the installation method differs. In this section you'll learn how to install the program on an Apple computer.

Whether you have a Mac or a PC, installing the *Our Family Archive* program on your computer is essential because the archive database cannot be added to or changed while it is stored on a CD-ROM disc. It needs to be on a hard drive, like the one built into your computer.

1 **Inserting the disc** Insert the CD into your computer's disc drive. You may need to momentarily hold down (don't just tap) the *Eject* button on the keyboard to open the CD tray, depending on the Macintosh model you are using.

2 **Launch the CD window** After a few moments an icon will appear on your computer's desktop. Double-click on it, and a new *Finder* window will appear with the license agreement and the *Our Family Archive* program.

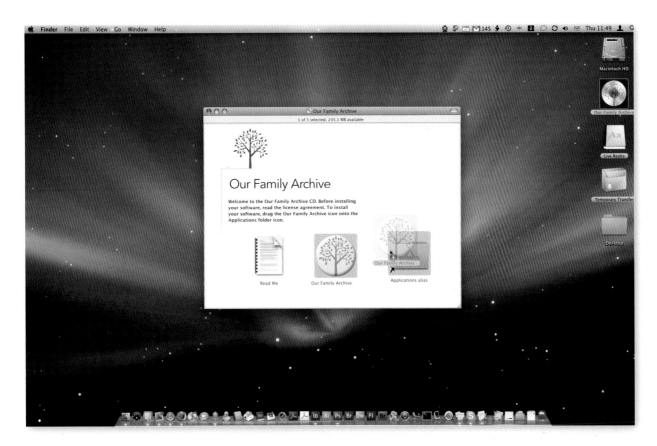

❸ Open the license agreement
Double-click on the Read Me PDF
file in the new window, and take
a moment to read it. To install *Our
Family Archive* in your computer's
main *Applications* folder, drag the
Our Family Archive icon onto the
Applications icon in the same folder.

If you prefer, you can install the
program in a different location
on your computer, or even in an
external hard drive. Just drag the
Our Family Archive icon to the
folder or disc in which you'd like
to install the program.

Tip://MacBook Air

Some Apple computer models,
such as the new, superthin
MacBook Air, come without a CD-
ROM drive in order to minimize
their size and weight. It's still
possible to install *Our Family
Archive* on such a computer, but
you will need access to either
an external CD-ROM drive or
another computer that does
have a CD-ROM drive.

If you have an external drive,
simply connect it to your
computer and follow the main
instructions. If you are using
another computer, you must
first install the remote disc
software on that computer (it
can be a Mac or PC). You can
then read the disc by selecting
the *Remote Disc* option from
the *Finder* window's sidebar
(the column of icons to the left).

How Our Family Archive Works

The program is arranged in pages and for every new relative or ancestor that you add to your archive, a new page is created that lets you see all of that individual's details. Each record is divided into two pages: a main page and a detail page.

BROWSE THE ARCHIVE ▶
VIEW THE FAMILY LIST ▶
CREATE AN ARCHIVE ▶

Our Family Archive

Using OUR FAMILY ARCHIVE you can store documents, photos and the recollections of family members and then print them out using beautifully designed, preformatted templates or you can play them as a slide show presentation. OUR FAMILY ARCHIVE puts you in charge of the project. Simply select from a wide range of template themes like Home and Garden, Sports, Military, Arts and Crafts, Work, etc., choose the text and images that you want to use and leave the rest to us.

Starting Point

The start-off point for the program is a simple home page from which you can access the list view, individual archive pages, or the link for adding a new record to the archive.

Archive Screens

There are several screens that you will become familiar with as you develop your family archive, including the *Browse*, *Create*, and *View* screens.

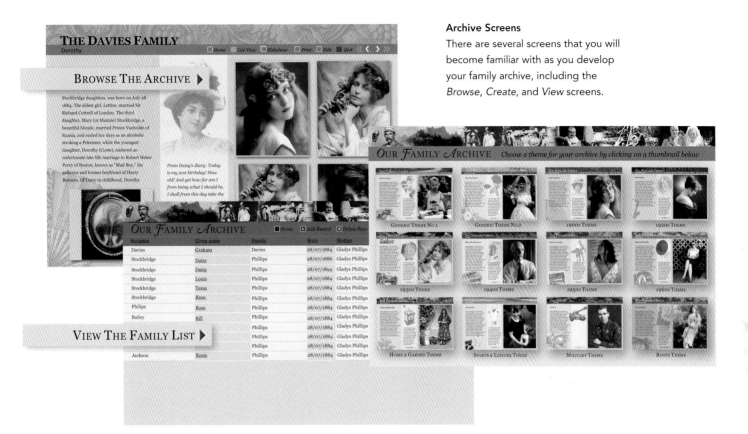

Toolbars

In addition to the links on the home page, there are toolbars visible on most of the pages (except the *Template Choice* screen). These also allow you to navigate within the program, either via the home page or directly from, for example, a record view to the list view. You also can move between records by clicking on the icons located at the right-hand end of the toolbar. The buttons on each toolbar are described in greater detail in the next chapter, but this illustration shows the main functions that you'll see on each page view.

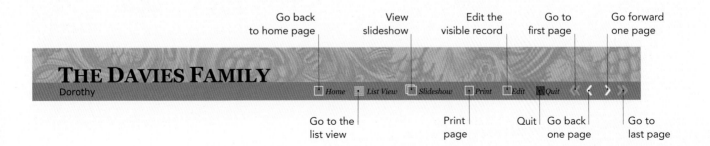

Our Family Archive Themes

In addition to compiling the details of a relative's or an ancestor's life in *Our Family Archive*, you also can choose from a dozen different design themes the one that best reflects the individual's personality or life history. The themes cover a broad spectrum of motifs and time periods, from your grandfather's war record to when your mother came of age in the 1950s.

How Themes Work

As you saw on page 52, information stored in the *Our Family Archive* program—such as a relative's details and photos—can be viewed in different ways. When you enter a new set of details (such as when you create a new record), they are added to the program's built-in database along with your choice of theme. The resulting archive page displays all of the details you entered in a layout that incorporates your chosen theme.

Layouts

Each new record you create can accommodate up to six pictures; you choose how many pictures you want to add. Even if you include the maximum six pictures in a relative's record, you can opt to display all or just some in the page view. You also can change the number of pictures that are displayed in the browsing view. The images that are not displayed will remain in the database until you replace or delete them.

OUR FAMILY ARCHIVE   *Choose a theme for your archive by clicking on a thumbnail below*

GENERIC THEME NO.1   GENERIC THEME NO.2   1900S THEME   1920S THEME

1930S THEME   1940S THEME   1950S THEME   1960S THEME

HOME & GARDEN THEME   SPORTS & LEISURE THEME   MILITARY THEME   ROOTS THEME

Theme Selection

The *Theme Creation* screen presents you with a simple choice of 12 design styles. Even after you've selected a theme for a new record, it's still possible to switch to another. There are more detailed instructions on selecting and changing themes in the next chapter.

Sample Layouts

There are 12 theme styles in the *Our Family Archive* program. Each one lets you choose from a range of layouts that can have from one to as many as six images on each page. Here are three examples:

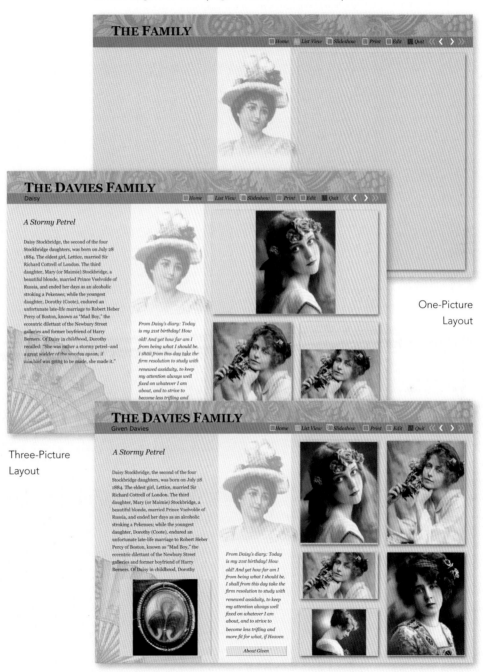

One-Picture Layout

Three-Picture Layout

Six-Picture Layout

Templates

Our Family Archive includes 12 templates that you can use as the background for a particular page or person. These range from generic themes that will be appropriate for most people to themes based on particular time periods or specific areas, such as military service or a strong interest in sports, for example.

Generic Theme No. 1

This clean, blue-green design features a group of five hot-air balloons, a rusting car, and a roadside scene behind the family name. This theme is the ideal choice for any car enthusiast. The aqua/turquoise toolbar background is reflected in the picture backings.

Generic Theme No. 2

This theme is decorated with flowers and petals. The pink scheme is traditionally feminine, although it would also be a good choice for an enthusiastic gardener, too.

1900s Theme

This design features a regal purple-and-teal color scheme—colors popular at the turn of the century. The pattern behind the family name and the fan reflect the intricate designs of the period.

1920s Theme

In many countries, the Roaring Twenties or the Jazz Age was an exciting time in which a booming economy helped dim memories of World War I and fueled a dynamic culture. The rich red colors of this design reflect the era's daring and flamboyance and provide a striking complement to the sepia-toned images.

→

1930s Theme

This theme is a little more somber, reflecting the difficulties of the decade that saw the struggle to escape the Great Depression. There was more to the 1930s, however, than grim economic realities. This was the decade in which the first LP was sold, and the design above the toolbar reflects the art of the era.

1940s Theme

The decade scarred by World War II, echoed by the military boots at the top of the page, was a period of great sacrifice and of progress, in which the foundations were laid for rapid post-war changes in technology, industry, housing, transportation, and culture.

1950s Theme

The politically conservative 1950s also were a very exciting time. In prosperous post-war North America, new suburbs boomed and television became mainstream. This was the decade when Elvis Presley and Johnny Cash rose to superstardom, and Australian opera diva Joan Sutherland made her debut in London's Covent Garden.

1960s Theme

This theme encompasses the period from the mid-'50s to the mid-'70s generally referred to as the Swinging Sixties. The '60s also saw a proliferation of exciting design work and, of course, this was the decade of the Apollo spaceflight program and the first lunar landing, the Beatles, the Peace Movement, Carnaby Street fashions, and "Free Love."

→

Home and Garden Theme

Families in which both parents work full-time are a relatively modern development. Many of your kin may have lived their whole lives at home, tending to house and family. This domestic theme incorporates images of trees and a traditional kitchen grinder.

Sports and Leisure Theme

This luscious green theme is ideal for anyone who enjoys the great outdoors, whether for a gentle stroll or a more active form of recreation. The stylized image behind the title area at the top depicts a golf course with a bunker to the right. If tennis isn't your thing, then choosing a six-picture layout will eliminate the tennis scene.

Military Theme

Service in the armed forces is an important event for many people, and this theme is designed to highlight that service. It incorporates a camouflage design and other miltary-related images.

Roots Theme

Harking back to a more distant era than many of the other themes, this theme works well with old sepia-toned images, such as the ones featured in its design. If you are able to track down and include more distant ancestors, this might be the best background for their pages.

GENERIC THEME No.1

GENERIC THEME No.2

1900s THEME

1930s THEME

1940s THEME

1950s THEME

HOME & GARDEN THEME

SPORTS & LEISURE THEME

MILITARY THEME

Using Our Family Archive

In the previous chapter, you learned how to install the *Our Family Archive* program and a bit about how it works. This chapter provides detailed, step-by-step instructions for the important tasks you will want to do, such as adding a new record for a family member or changing information you've already input.

You can think of this chapter as the manual for *Our Family Archive*, although the emphasis is on completing tasks, rather than highlighting features. By following the instructions in these pages, you will be able to transfer your research from paper to the screen and bring your family archive to life. You can then browse the pages and show and share them with family and friends.

Making Your First Entry

As you saw in the previous chapter, the *Our Family Archive* program is arranged into pages, one for each relative or ancestor you wish to include. Here are step-by-step instructions for adding a new page to your archive.

1 Launch the program
From either the *Start* menu (Windows) or the *Applications* folder (Mac), click on the *Our Family Archive* program to launch it. The program's home page will list three options. Click on *Create an Archive*.

2 Pick a theme As discussed on pages 60–67, you can choose from 12 different design templates, or themes, for each new page you add to your archive. To select a theme, click on its thumbnail in the next screen. For this sample page we've selected the roots theme.

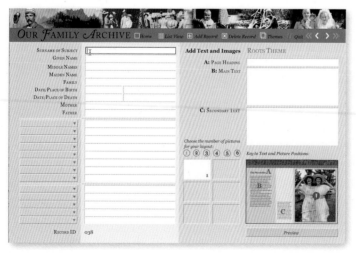

3 The detail input page As soon as you click on your choice of theme, the Input screen will appear. This is where you can enter all the details you know about the relative you're adding to the archive. The most important part of any entry, of course, is the person's name, so click in the empty white area next to the *Surname of Subject* label. This makes the area, called a *field*, ready for editing, and a flashing cursor indicates where your text will appear.

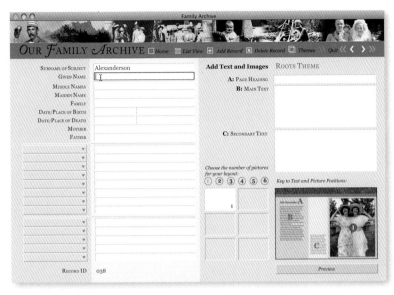

4 Entering names Type your relative's last name in the field. If you make a mistake while typing, you can use the Delete or Backspace keys to go back over the name and retype it. Once you have input the last name, click in the field directly below it, labeled *Given Name*, and type the person's first name. Once you click on another field, the information you've entered in the previous field is automatically stored in the archive. Input all of the person's names that you know of, and don't worry if you have to leave a field blank—*Maiden Name*, for example, won't necessarily apply to everyone.

5 Adding the date and place of birth If you know when and where your relative was born, click on the left side of the empty fields labeled *Date of Birth* and *Place of Birth*. To input the date, click on the field as you did with the name fields, but don't type in anything. A small calendar icon will appear in the field after you have clicked on it. Click on this icon to open the *Date Entry* tool. Simply click on the up/down arrows to select the year and on the left/right ones until the correct month is displayed, then pick the day. The *Place of Birth* field, however, allows you to type in this information directly, as you did with the name fields.

6 Other fields In addition, the *Input* screen also includes labeled fields for your relative's date of death and parents' names, as well as a group of unlabeled fields in which you can input the names of the subject's spouse and children and other details of her life. Our sample subject, Jayne Alexanderson, is married—a fact worth noting—so click on the arrow to the right of the first unlabeled field and select *Married To* from the drop-down menu that appears.

→

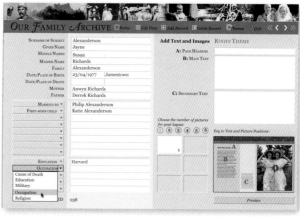

❼ Adding the names of spouses and children Click on the field that is now labeled *Married To*, and enter the name of your relative's spouse. There are seven other fields in which you can input the names of spouses and children by choosing from the drop-down menu.

❽ More flexible fields Beneath the eight fields for spouses and children are another five that work in a similar way, but you can choose the field title using a drop-down menu. Pick *Education*, for instance, to record the name of your relative's school or college.

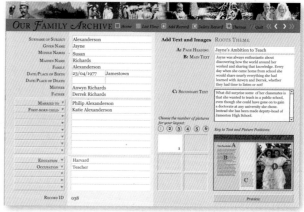

❾ Your relative's story Facts and figures are important, but they don't tell the whole story of a person's life. That's why the first page of each archive you create includes space for several paragraphs of text as well as photos. To input your relative's story, start by entering a title of your choice in the field labeled *Page Title*, located toward the top right-hand side of the page.

❿ Writing the main and secondary text To write about your relative, click in the larger *Main Text* or *Secondary Text* fields and type. When you reach the bottom of the field, you may continue to type; if you do so, you can use the *Scroll* bar that will appear to move the text up and down as needed. Keep the main text to about 100 words; the secondary text to about 60 words.

⓫ Selecting the layout In addition to text, you can add pictures to your new page. But first you have to select a layout from among six options, depending on the number of pictures you want to include. If you just have two, as in the example above, click on the 2 button just above the six rectangular picture fields. You'll notice that two of the rectangles are now lit up and the example design to the right now contains two numbered pictures.

⓬ Adding your pictures To add the pictures to your archive, click on the numbered rectangles. The number in the lower right-hand corner of the rectangle corresponds to the numbered example photo in the example design to the right. So to place a picture in area 1, click on the rectangle numbered 1, and choose the picture using the familiar operating system dialog box. Repeat the process for the second picture.

The finished entry
Once you have entered your data and images, click the *Preview* button on the bottom right to see the new page with text and images in place and in the format that you chose. To see the details, click the *About Jayne* button beneath the secondary text.

Browsing the Records

Once you've created records for two or more relatives, you can use the program to browse through them all. Each relative's record constitutes a new page and clicking on the arrows takes you from one page to the next or directly to the first or last pages.

BROWSE THE ARCHIVE ▶
VIEW THE FAMILY LIST ▶
CREATE AN ARCHIVE ▶

Our Family Archive

Using OUR FAMILY ARCHIVE you can store documents, photos and the recollections of family members and then print them out using beautifully designed, preformatted templates or you can play them as a slide show presentation. OUR FAMILY ARCHIVE puts you in charge of the project. Simply select from a wide range of template themes like Home and Garden, Sports, Military, Arts and Crafts, Work, etc., choose the text and images that you want to use and leave the rest to us.

❶ Opening the *Browse* mode To access the *Browse* mode, click the *Browse the Archive* button on the home page or the *Browse* button in the toolbar if the screen you are viewing features one.

❷ The first page When you switch to the *Browse* mode via the home page, you will be taken to the first record that you created. To view a different page, use the single white arrows near the top right-hand corner of the page. Click on the right-pointing arrow to turn to the next page, and on the left-pointing arrow to view the previous page.

3 **The last page** Next to the single arrows are left- and right-facing double arrows that take you directly to the first or last page of the archive. Clicking on the right-facing double arrows will bring up the record you added most recently (the last page of your archive), whereas the left-facing double arrows will take you back to the first page. If nothing happens when you click on a double arrow, you're already on the first or last record.

4 **More details** When you reach a page you've been searching for, click on the *About...* button at the bottom of the page. This brings up the second page of the record with your relative's biographical details and just one photo (the first one you added to the record). The *Toolbar* buttons work the same way on either page, allowing you to browse back and forth between records.

Toggling Between Pages

Each record has two pages—a main page with introductory text and all the photos you added to the record, and a second page with biographical details and just one photo. At the bottom of each page in a record, there's always a button that allows you to switch between

the two. The arrows in the toolbar at the top of the page will take you to a different record, and the program will always show the main page—with the intro text and all of the photos—first.

Finding a Specific Entry

Browsing the archive and reminiscing about your relatives can be fun, but what if you want to go straight to the page for a particular relative? In this case, you need to launch the *Our Family Archive* program's *List* view.

    The *List* view shows the names, dates of birth, parents, and record IDs for all the relatives you've added to the archive and enables you to access each individual's record directly. This list can be sorted by any of the previously mentioned criteria, making it easier to find a particular record. Once you've found the record you want, you can view the page in *Browse* mode or edit any of the details in the record (see pages 78–81 for instructions).

❶ Launching the list To launch the *List* view, click the *View the Family List* button, or click the *List view* from the *Browse* or *Edit* views. A complete list of every entry in the archive will appear on your screen.

❷ Sorting by last name When you create a new record, it is added to the archive sequentially and assigned a record ID number in ascending order. When you launch the *List* view, the entries are sorted by their record ID numbers, which appear on the far right of each entry. However, it's often more useful to sort the list alphabetically by surname. To do that, just click on *Surname* in the title bar at the top of the list.

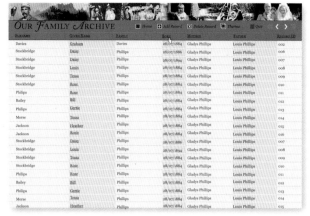

3 **Sorting by birth date** To make the search for a relative's record even easier, you may want to sort the list by date of birth rather than surname, since so many of your relatives are likely to have the same last name. To resort the list, click on *Born* in the title bar.

4 **Scrolling the list** As you add records the entries in the *List* view may eventually get too long to fit on your computer screen. When that happens, use the window's scroll bar to scroll up and down the list. When you locate the entry you're looking for, click on the person's name to open the *Edit* view.

Tip://quick theme change

If you'd like to change the theme you've selected for a record, click on the record in the *List* view but not on the blue highlighted given name link. A small black marker will appear to the left of the entry. When it does, click on *Themes* on the toolbar and you will be able to pick a new theme for that record.

5 **The *Edit* view** In the *Edit* view you can review and update all of the information for that particular relative (see pages 78–81). If you just want to view the finished page rather than change anything on it, click the *Preview* button to bring up the page in the *Browse* mode.

Editing Entries

In the course of your research, it's likely that you'll turn up more information about a relative whose record you've already created. You might even find an error that needs correcting. In either case, it's easy to change information in the archive at any time. To edit a page, you first have to locate it, either through the *Browse* or the *List* view, as described on pages 74–77. In the following example we use the *Browse* mode.

1 Identifying the problem entry
Once you've found the entry you're looking for and identified a detail that needs updating, click the *Edit* button in the toolbar.

2 Adding a new detail The *Edit* button takes you to the familiar data-entry page you used to create a new record. To update it with new information, such as the birth of a second child, click on the drop-down button and pick *Second-Born Child* from the menu.

3 Adding new text To type in the name of the newborn child, click in the text field next to the title you added and type in a name. Continue to add whatever new information you have to the other empty fields.

④ Making text ready for editing You also can change the text you've already input in any of the text fields. If you want to edit the main text, for example, just click at the point in the text where you want to start making changes. The text area will be selected, and a cursor will appear.

⑤ Editing text When the text area is highlighted, you can move the cursor using the arrow keys (also known as cursor keys) on your computer keyboard. The *Backspace* button deletes characters behind (to the left of) the cursor; the *Delete* key works in the opposite direction.

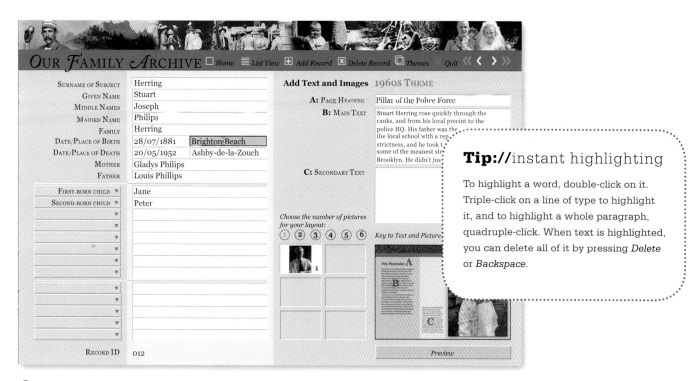

Tip://instant highlighting

To highlight a word, double-click on it. Triple-click on a line of type to highlight it, and to highlight a whole paragraph, quadruple-click. When text is highlighted, you can delete all of it by pressing *Delete* or *Backspace*.

⑥ Replacing text If you want to replace all of the text in a particular field, like an erroneous place of birth, just double-click on the field to highlight all the text. As soon as you begin typing, the text will be replaced.

→

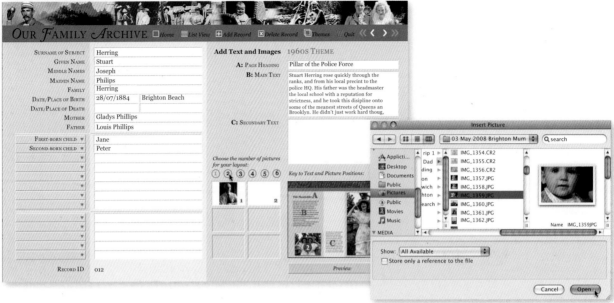

7 Making room for more pictures To add an additional picture, you have to alter the layout to increase the number of available picture spaces. To do that, just click the circular number button on the right side of the screen. For example, if you want to add one new picture to a layout that already has one, click the 2 button.

8 Adding the picture Click on the white picture rectangle to open the computer's *Explorer* (Windows) or *Finder* (Mac) window, and use this to locate the picture you want to include.

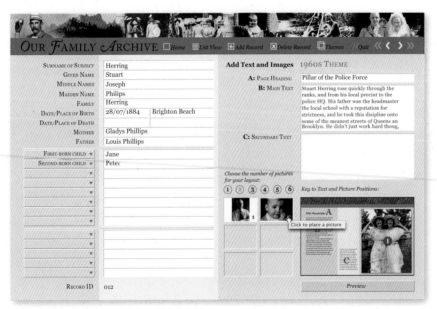

9 Replacing a picture You also can replace one of the pictures in your layout with another. Just click on the small numbered thumbnail of the picture you want to replace to open the picture selection dialog box.

THE HERRING FAMILY
Stuart Herring

Home · List View · Slideshow · Print · Edit · Quit

Pillar of the Police Force

Stuart Herring rose quickly through the ranks, and from his local precinct to the police HQ. His father was the headmaster of the local school with a reputation for strictness, and he took this discipline onto some of the meanest streets of Queens and Brooklyn. He didn't just work hard though, he played hard too. He played gigs at rock clubs across the city, and had quite a reputation.

About Stuart

Preview the page
The previous steps allow you to alter the information stored in the *Our Family Archive* database. Once you have finished editing, click *Preview* to review your changes in the *Browse* view.

Subtracting a Picture

If you change your mind about including a picture, you also can reduce the number of pictures in your layout. Just click a lower number button to alter the layout. However, this does not delete the image from the archive—you can restore it whenever you like.

Switching Themes

Pages 78–81 explored different ways of extending or updating the data in the archive. The only remaining thing you may want to change is the page's theme. There are two ways to achieve this, although both use the same familiar tools.

From the *Edit* View

① **Click the *Theme* button** When you're working on the *Edit* view, click the *Theme* button in the toolbar.

② **Choose your theme** Using the familiar theme thumbnail page, select your new choice of theme.

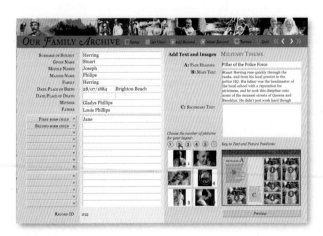

③ **Edit mode** Once you've picked a theme, you will be taken to the *Edit* mode, where you can make any additional changes. If you're happy with the details, go straight to the next step.

④ **Finish** Click the *Preview* button to return back to the page in the *Browser* view, resplendent in its new theme.

From the *List* View

1 Highlight the record When you're in the *List* mode you can highlight a record by clicking on it.

2 Go to theme choice The selected record is indicated with a small black marker to the left. All the other records have a small white area to the left of their list entries.

3 Pick a theme Choose a theme, as described in step 2 on the opposite page, and follow the remaining steps.

4 Back to the list To return to the *List* view, where you started, click the *List* button in the toolbar.

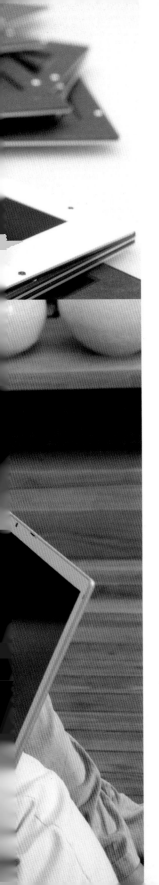

Showing and Sharing Your Archive

Once you start exploring your heritage and recording the details of your ancestors' and relatives' lives in the *Our Family Archive* database, you'll inevitably get the urge to share your work with others so they can see it, enjoy it, and perhaps even be encouraged to join in the fun. If you're lucky, other family members will want to swap details with you as they start their own archive and, in the process, help keep your legwork down to a minimum!

This chapter will also show you all the ways you can make copies for your own needs, especially for backup purposes. While backing up your work is not a glamorous subject, it is increasingly important as more of our lives are recorded digitally and things can—and sometimes do—go wrong with computers.

On the following pages you will find clear and simple instructions for viewing slideshows, making a digital backup, and printing out a page or a list. You'll also learn how to protect your prints and discs so they last for many decades.

Slideshows

Our Family Archive has a built-in slideshow function that lets you display your pictures in sequence, sharply and clearly, on your computer screen. The slideshow viewer is directly accessible from any page of the browser and it is very easy to use.

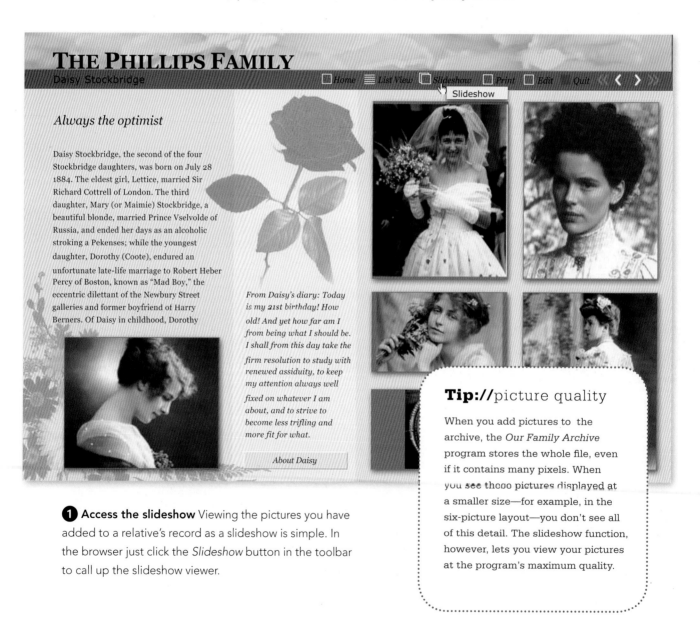

THE PHILLIPS FAMILY

Daisy Stockbridge

☐ *Home* ≡ *List View* ☐ *Slideshow* ☐ *Print* ☐ *Edit* *Quit* ‹ ›

Slideshow

Always the optimist

Daisy Stockbridge, the second of the four Stockbridge daughters, was born on July 28 1884. The eldest girl, Lettice, married Sir Richard Cottrell of London. The third daughter, Mary (or Maimie) Stockbridge, a beautiful blonde, married Prince Vselvolde of Russia, and ended her days as an alcoholic stroking a Pekenses; while the youngest daughter, Dorothy (Coote), endured an unfortunate late-life marriage to Robert Heber Percy of Boston, known as "Mad Boy," the eccentric dilettant of the Newbury Street galleries and former boyfriend ot Harry Berners. Of Daisy in childhood, Dorothy

From Daisy's diary: Today is my 21st birthday! How old! And yet how far am I from being what I should be. I shall from this day take the firm resolution to study with renewed assiduity, to keep my attention always well fixed on whatever I am about, and to strive to become less trifling and more fit for what.

About Daisy

① Access the slideshow Viewing the pictures you have added to a relative's record as a slideshow is simple. In the browser just click the *Slideshow* button in the toolbar to call up the slideshow viewer.

Tip://picture quality

When you add pictures to the archive, the *Our Family Archive* program stores the whole file, even if it contains many pixels. When you see these pictures displayed at a smaller size—for example, in the six-picture layout—you don't see all of this detail. The slideshow function, however, lets you view your pictures at the program's maximum quality.

THE PHILLIPS FAMILY
Daisy Stockbridge

Home   List View   Slideshow   Print   Edit   Quit   ‹ ›

Play Slideshow

Always the optimist

Daisy Stockbridge, the second of the four Stockbridge daughters, was born on July 28 1884. The eldest girl, Lettice, married Sir Richard Cottrell of London. The third daughter, Mary (or Maimie) Stockbridge, a beautiful blonde, married Prince Vselvolde of Russia, and ended her days as an alcoholic stroking a Pekenese; while the youngest daughter, Dorothy (Coote), endured an unfortunate late-life marriage to Robert Heber Percy of Boston, known as "Mad Boy," the eccentric dilettant of the Newbury Street galleries and former boyfriend of Harry Berners. Of Daisy in childhood, Dorothy

From Daisy's diary: Today is my 21st birthday! How old! And yet how far am I from being what I should be. I shall from this day take the firm resolution to study with renewed assiduity, to keep my attention always well fixed on whatever I am about, and to strive to become less trifling and more fit for what.

About Daisy

2 **Enjoy the slideshow** The screen switches to a black background and displays the pictures you have added to that relative's record in sequence. The computer will automatically change the picture after a few seconds.

3 **Return to the archive** The pictures will cycle in a continuous loop until you want to return to the archive. Once you are finished viewing, click the *Back* button at the bottom of the screen, and you will be returned to the browser.

Backing Up to a Disc

Building up your family archive requires a fairly large investment of time, so you'll want to protect your archive against possible damage or loss. It's an unfortunate fact that all computers are susceptible to failure. That's why it's important to keep a copy—known as a backup—of your database that you can store separately from the original.

Almost all computers come with an optical media drive—either a CD, DVD, or Blu-ray drive. The blank discs are relatively cheap and, once you've saved data on them, they can be safely stored away from your computer.

How you decide to back up to a disc depends on several things—whether your computer is an Apple Mac or a Windows-based PC; instructions for both operating systems are listed below. The instructions for Windows Vista also apply to Windows XP.

Windows Vista (PC)

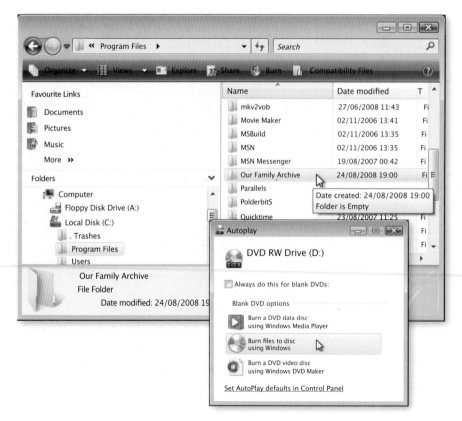

1 Close the program To copy the archive to a disc or any other media, first make sure the *Our Family Archive* program is not in use. Quit the program by clicking the *Close* icon or by choosing *Quit* from the *File* menu in the toolbar.

2 Insert a blank disc Place a blank CD or DVD in your computer drive. Your computer will recognize the disc after a few moments and offer a number of options. Select *Burn Files to Disc*.

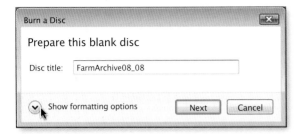

3 Name the disc Before copying your archive to the disc, give the disc a name. The name should be practical and no longer than the maximum 16 characters allowed. It is a good idea to include an abbreviated month and year. Once you have named the disc, click on the *Formatting Options* icon.

4 Maximize the disc's compatibility To make the disc compatible with as many drives as possible, it is best to make it a single-session or "write once" disc. Choose *Mastered* from the pop-up menu, and then click *Next*.

Tips://write once or multisession?

- The process of copying and saving data on a CD or DVD is called burning a disc. You can format discs so you can record data onto them only once or rerecord multiple times. Some CD-ROM drives can read only single-session discs, so for maximum compatibility with different drives, choose the single-session option. The downside to this is that you'll need a new disc each time you back up your archive, even if the file doesn't use up all the space on the old disc.

- An alternative is to format the disc so you can save to it more than once. The instructions in this section are for single-session discs. However, if you expect to use the disc only with your current or newer computers, consider the multisession option. Window's default Live File System (multisession) lets you keep updating the files on the disc until it runs out of space.

5 Locate the *Our Family Archive* program An Explorer window will appear on your screen, allowing you to locate the *Our Family Archive* program and select it to be burned onto the disc. First click on the [C:] icon in the sidebar to select the disc drive where your programs are stored.

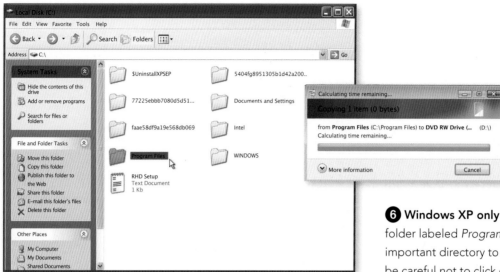

6 **Windows XP only** Double-click on the folder labeled *Program Files*. This is an important directory to your computer, so be careful not to click on any files other than those mentioned here.

7 **Select the Archive** Click once on the directory labeled *Our Family Archive* to highlight it, and then click *Burn* in the toolbar. This copies the *Our Family Archive* program files to the CD or DVD-ROM.

8 **Close session** Right-click on the CD or DVD icon in the sidebar to the left of the window. Choose *Close Session* from the drop-down menu.

Tips://archival media

- Although optical discs are convenient and much more durable than the discs and tapes that preceded them, it would be optimistic to expect something so cheap to last forever. In fact, CDs and DVDs will start to degrade after a few years, but potentially much sooner if you do not keep discs in a suitable place. The weak spot is at the edges of the disc, where the recording layer can be exposed to moisture, causing visible damage.

- Good-quality, branded archival discs are more durable, and if you store your discs away from moisture and light, they can be expected to last more than 100 years. If your living conditions aren't quite like the dry desert caves that preserved the Dead Sea Scrolls for 2,000 years, the best option is to copy the disc's contents onto a new disc every few years. This approach also has the advantage of ensuring that your discs will be compatible with the most recent generation of computers.

Mac

1 Getting started Make sure you have quit the *Our Family Archive* program, and then insert a blank disc into your Mac's disc drive. After a few moments the disc will be recognized, and you will be offered a number of choices. Choose *Open Finder* and then click *OK*.

2 Opening the *Burn* folder An icon labeled *Untitled Disc* will appear on the desktop. Double-click on it to open a special finder window called a *Burn* folder. This folder acts like any other except that when you drag files into it, links are created rather than copies. The files remain in their original locations.

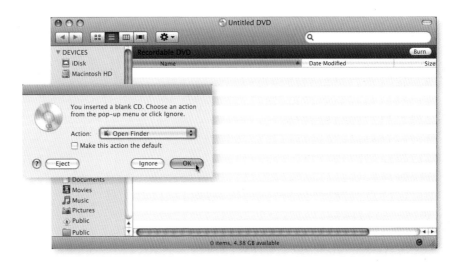

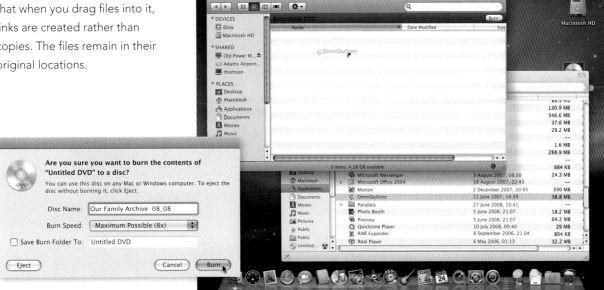

3 Adding the archive From the Finder, press *Apple+N* to open another Finder window, and then select the *Applications* icon from the sidebar to see all of your programs. Find your copy of *Our Family Archive*, and drag its folder from the *Applications* folder to the *Burn* folder.

4 Burning a disc You can add as many other files as you like to the *Burn* folder, such as spare photos or videos. When you are ready, click the *Burn* button in the toolbar at the top of the folder contents. In the window that pops up, give your disc a name, then click *OK* to begin the burning process.

Other Ways to Back Up

Recording your archive to a durable optical disc is a useful way of backing up your work or sharing it with a friend or relative. It is not, however, the only way. The options described in this section differ in how they balance cost and speed.

An important factor to consider is whether you want to back up just your family archive or perform system-wide backups of other files on your computer. If you want to perform a system-wide back up, then you need plenty of gigabytes of storage space and the cost-per-gigabyte becomes more important. If it's just your family archive that you want to back up, then all you need to consider is the cost of sufficient storage for your expanding archive. It is unlikely that this will ever to get much larger than a couple of gigabytes, so DVDs are ideal.

USB Sticks

A USB stick is a flash-memory data-storage device that plugs into a computer's universal serial bus (USB) port. These drives come in many different designs and often are compact and durable enough to be carried around on a keychain or in a pocket.

They all share the same basic file system, and copying to a USB stick is very straightforward. Another advantage is that it is rewriteable, so you don't have to worry about whether you should use write-once or multisession modes.

1 Insert the USB stick Before you can write to a USB stick, you have to insert it into a free USB port on your computer. USB ports are often found on the back of a computer, but also look for them on the sides and front, or even on the keyboard or monitor.

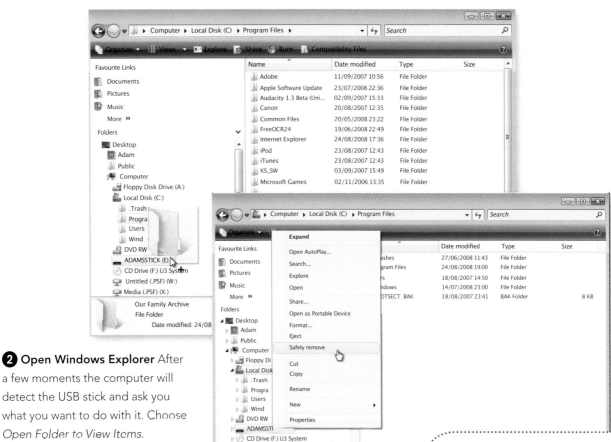

2 Open Windows Explorer After a few moments the computer will detect the USB stick and ask you what you want to do with it. Choose *Open Folder to View Items*.

3 Using Windows Explorer An Explorer window much like the one shown in Step 5 of the Windows Vista CD/DVD-burning instructions on page 89 will appear. Click once on *C:*, open the *Program Files* folder, and drag the *Our Family Archive* folder onto the USB stick's drive number or letter. In this case it is drive *E:* and is called *ADAMSSTICK*.

4 Removing the USB stick Once your files have been copied, right-click on the USB stick's drive name in the *Explorer* window and select *Remove Safely* from the list. This ensures that all file operations are complete so that you don't damage data by pulling out the stick too soon. After a moment a message appears, advising you can remove the drive from the computer.

Tip://sticks on a Mac

Using a USB stick with a Mac is very easy. If you put the stick into a spare USB socket on your computer or keyboard, it will appear on your desktop as an external drive. To copy your files, locate the *Our Family Archive* folder in your *Applications* folder and drag it onto the USB stick-drive icon. Once the files have been copied, drag the USB stick's icon to the trash (which will have changed to *Eject*) and the icon will be removed from the desktop. You can now remove the USB stick.

External Hard Drives

You can back up your archive to an external hard drive in much the same way as to a USB stick. Both types of storage device plug into a computer's USB port, although some external hard drives will also connect via a FireWire port, which is a faster connection.

Unlike a USB stick, an external hard drive generally requires its own power supply. Because of its greater storage capacity, you can use an external hard drive to do a complete backup of your computer system. This means that you can retrieve an individual file or your entire system from the external drive if something goes wrong with your computer. Automated backup software enables your computer— whether it's an Apple Mac or a Windows-based PC— to make automatic backups to an external hard drive. Connecting the hard drive to the computer and powering it up triggers the backup utilities. The Mac utility is called *Time Machine*, and it is built in to the Leopard version of Mac OS X. The Windows equivalent is the *Back Up and Restore* tool.

Online Backup

By harnessing the speed of the Internet, it is now possible for you to back up your files without investing in any new hardware at all. Online services, such as *www.ibackup.com*, use extremely fast broadband connections to back up your most important files to a remote computer. The following step-by-step instructions are based on the *ibackup* system, but they are very similar to those for other systems. Before you can get started, you need to set up an account with the backup service and download and install its software. After that, the process of backing up is simple.

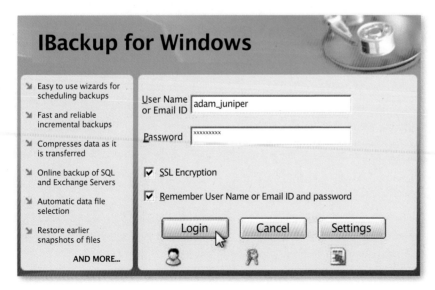

1 Log In Run the *ibackup* program from your Windows *Start* menu (or the Mac OS X *Applications* folder). Enter the user name and password that you chose when setting up your account.

2 **Select your files** Because online services usually have a limited amount of space, they usually protect only vital folders. To indicate that the *Our Family Archive* folder needs to be included among those you want backed up, check it in the directory tree. You will find it in *C:>Program Files*.

3 **Make a backup** The program will automatically make contact with the server and back up your files once a day. To make an immediate backup, click the *Back Up Now* button in the lower left.

4 **Restore files** If you need to restore your files to an earlier state (recover them from the backup), open the directory tree in the right-hand window. This shows the backup files on the remote server. Check the *Our Family Archive* files, and press the *Restore* button on the lower-right side of the screen.

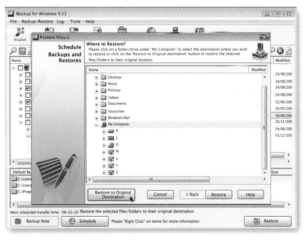

5 **Replace files** To replace the files in the original location, choose *Restore to Original Destination* and the archive will be restored to the state it was in at the last backup.

Printers and Printing

Up until very recently there were a number of printing technologies available for home or office use, including dye-sublimation and laser printers. Today, however, the ink-jet printer is king, at least in the home. Dye-sublimation (dye-sub) printers are more expensive to operate, but have found a niche in direct-to-print digital photography because the quality of the output is very close to traditional photographic prints. At the lower end of the price scale, color laser printers are better suited to office environments where their ability to handle a heavy workload quickly is more important than producing the highest-quality prints.

Ink-jet printers, on the other hand, now dominate the home, photographic print, and small business markets because of their quality and adaptability. An ink-jet printer is ideally suited to printing pages or photos from your family archive. The basic technology is the same for all ink-jets—tiny bubbles of ink are sprayed onto the page, where they mix to give the impression of many more shades of color.

Standard Ink-jet

A standard-quality ink-jet-printer is very inexpensive to buy and relatively cheap to operate. To keep costs down, these machines use just three inks—cyan, magenta, and yellow—to re-create most other colors. The three inks are mixed together to create black when it is needed, but this tends to result in muddy, dark brown prints. Models that also include black ink produce better prints; they may cost more, but they're generally worth it.

Standard ink-jet printers are flexible and will capably handle any task you ask of them. However, they do not excel when it comes to speed, and they aren't the best for printing photographs. Another drawback with some models is that their ink tanks are combined in a single disposable cartridge, so when one color runs out, you have to replace the entire cartridge, which isn't very cost-effective.

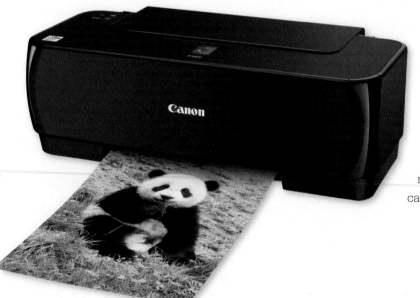

Photo Ink-jet

If you're interested in making high-quality prints of your photographs, it's worth investing in a printer designed for that purpose. Although the line between a standard-ink-jet and a photo-ink-jet is somewhat arbitrary—the technology is basically the same for both—photo models have many refinements that dramatically boost print quality. A photo printer often includes additional inks, which means it can create more shades, and the ink dots sprayed on the page are smaller, so they are less obvious to the eye and pictures appear sharper.

All-in-One Printer Scanners

A scanner is a very useful tool for a project such as *Our Family Archive*. Realizing that space is limited, many manufacturers have conveniently combined a printer and a scanner into a single device. These multifunctional units are well worth investigating, especially if you sometimes need to copy documents, because they also can act as copiers without the computer's assistance.

Printer terminology

Ink droplet size is measured in picoliters (one 1,000,000,000,000th of a liter). The smaller the amount, the smaller the size of the ink droplet that is sprayed on the paper, so the higher the level of detail.

Printer speed is measured in Pages Per Minute (PPM), although the speed quoted by most manufactures is the lowest quality mode used for printing text documents on Letter or A4 sized paper, rather than the time taken to print high quality photos. The printer will work considerably slower in its best quality mode.

Dots Per Inch (DPI) is a measure of the printer's resolution; the higher the better. The dots referred to are the individual ink dots the printer users, rather than the many millions of colors possible on screen, so DPI is a different measure from Pixels Per Inch (PPI), the measure you will see in graphics programs.

Archival Paper and Inks

There are three main reasons to print pages from *Our Family Archive:* to have copies to show and share in your home, to give copies to friends or relatives, or to simply make a hard-copy record of the archive. For this last reason you'll want your printed records to be as long-lasting as possible. Here's how can you make this happen.

Just as the never-ending stream of cosmetics advertisements on our TV screens remind us, the best solution is to combat the signs of aging. Without getting too technical, scientists have found that the acid content of paper leads to its eventual degradation, so modern papers are balanced with an alkaline reserve. This gives them, in ideal conditions, a theoretical lifetime of up to 1,000 years. In practice, however, things don't always work out that way.

Archival Paper

All good modern paper is nonacidic. This helps prevent the lignin in the wood pulp that makes up the paper from turning it yellow and brittle over time. Archival paper is more than just nonacidic; it is slightly alkaline, which boosts its antiacidic qualities and its resistance to age-related yellowing and brittleness. But it is important that you buy archival paper specifically tailored to ink-jet printers—and preferably to your brand of printer. Only ink-jet–coated papers will fully absorb the ink and prevent spreading for a clean, sharp result.

Tip://storing printed documents

As mentioned on page 90, the Dead Sea Scrolls
lasted so long because they were kept from their
two main enemies—moisture and light. The same
is true of modern printed documents; most paper
manufacturers' claims of lifetime durability are based
on the assumption that the documents will be framed
under glass and kept out of direct light. While this
might suit photographs, it is unlikely you will want to
frame printouts of your family-archive prints, so think
about keeping them in a photograph album where you
can display the pages and look through them whenever
you want. If they start to fade, you can always print
them out again.

Archival Inks

If you want your ink-jet printout to
last, you also need to be sure that you
use archival inks. These are usually
formulated to work hand-in-hand with
the manufacturer's archival papers. Like
archival paper, archival ink is slightly
alkaline to combat the effects of
atmospheric acidity. As a result,
archival ink resists fading far longer
than regular ink.

Print Setup

Before you can print any document, it's important that you perform a print setup. This tells the computer how to set up the document so it will fit onto the printed page correctly.

Adjusting the settings before you print is especially important with *Our Family Archive* because the *Main Page* and *List* views have to be oriented differently in order to print them out properly. As a result, you'll need to change settings when you switch from one view to another.

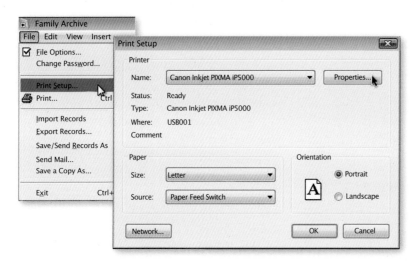

❶ Opening *Print Setup* As in most applications with print capability, the *Print Setup* dialog in *Our Family Archive* is accessed by clicking *File>Print Setup.*

❷ Checking the printer Even if you have only one printer, your computer—especially if it's a laptop—will probably include configuration details for other printers. Make sure your printer's correct name and connection information appear in the *Print Setup* dialog, then click *Properties.*

❸ *Page Setup* tab The main *Properties* screen shows you details about the paper and quality that you can revisit before each individual print job. The important details can be found under the *Page Setup* tab.

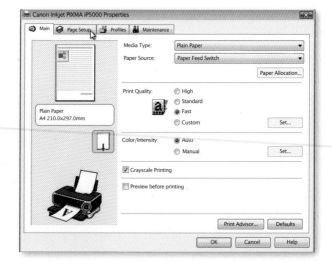

4 Page sizes Most printer software drivers can scale a page up or down in size so that you get the best possible fit on the page. That means describing the virtual measurements using the *Custom* option under *Page Size*.

5 Measurements Set up your page with a width of 9.6 inches (24 cm) and a height of 13.3 inches (34 cm). These dimensions allow you to fit a single page of an archive on one sheet.

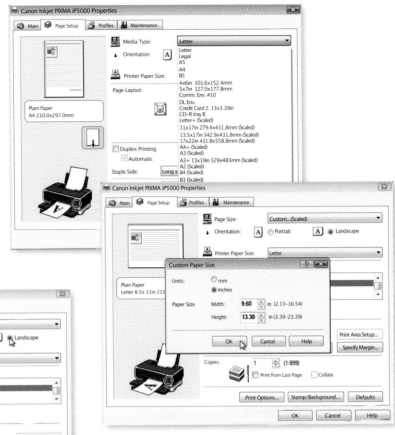

6 *Landscape* Because the design of *Our Family Archive* is landscape—like your monitor—check the *Landscape* orientation button.

7 *Fit to Page* The *Printer Paper Size* is the size of the paper in your printer. Once you select the paper size (Letter or A4 are most common), your computer should automatically select the *Fit to Page* option, which scales the archive record page to fit the paper. Click *OK* to confirm your printer settings. You are now ready to print your page.

Printing a Page

You can print any page of your family archive with a home or office printer. Thanks to the high resolution of most desktop printers, you'll be able to see all the details on the printed page that you can see on your computer screen. All you have to do before printing is check and adjust the print setup, as described on pages 100–101.

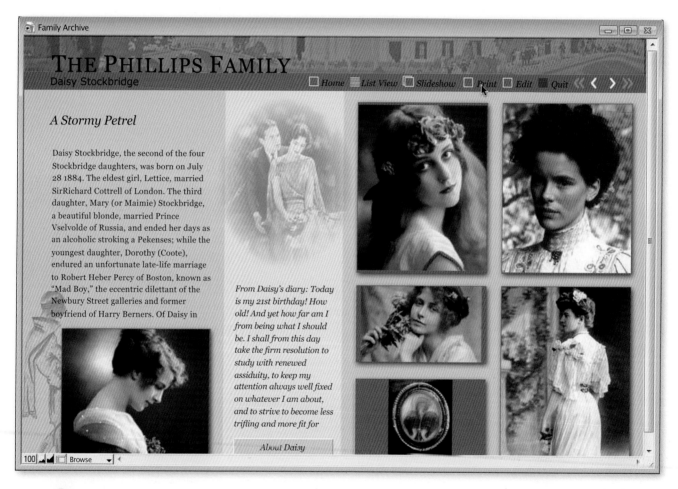

❶ Choose a page Browse to the page you want to print using the *Browser* view, or skip to it using the *List* view, then click the *Print* button in the toolbar.

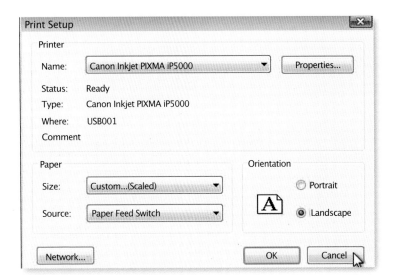

2 **Print a single record** At the top of the *Print* dialog box is a small drop-down menu labeled *Print*. Click on it, and select *Current Record*.

3 **Checking the *Print Setup*** Click the *Properties* button and make sure that the *Paper Size* indicated in the lower left is correct. Click *Cancel* if you're happy with the settings.

> **Tip://**paper types
>
> If you are using a different paper type than the default "plain paper"—for example, high-quality archival paper—you will need to alter the *Media Type* and *Print Quality* options under the *Main* tab.

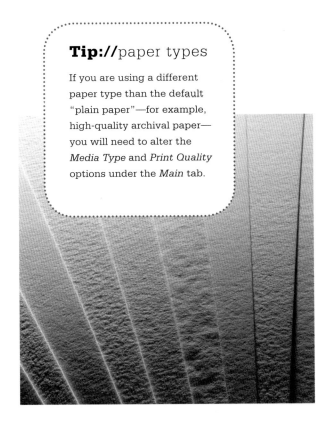

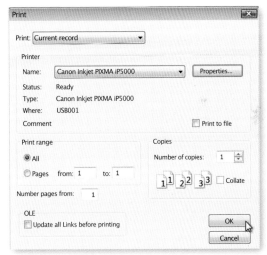

4 **Begin printing** The *Print* dialog box will appear again. Make sure that the printer is switched on and that it has paper. Click *OK*, and after a few moments the printer will start to operate. The delay may be slightly longer than usual as the computer scales the archive page to match the paper size.

Printing Lists

In addition to printing from the *Page* view in *Our Family Archive*, you also can print from the *List* view, which allows you to fit a lot of relatives' names and basic details on a single sheet of paper. The list printout can serve as a useful index and reference when, for example, you're doing research away from your computer.

Before you print a list, you need to decide whether to print it in landscape mode, like the page shown on page 102, or in portrait mode (see box, page 105). If you switch to portrait mode, you will be able to fit more information on a page, but you'll have to enter a new custom paper size before you print.

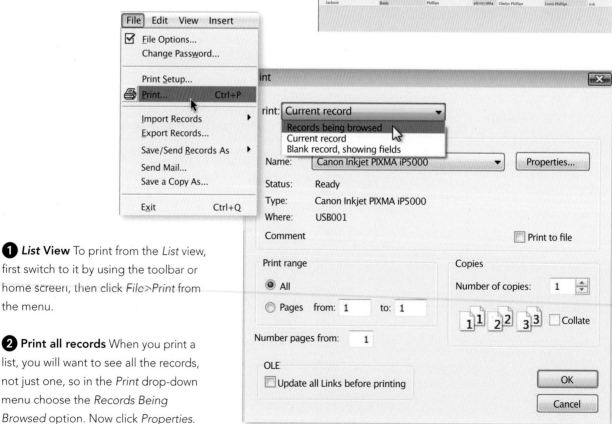

❶ *List* **View** To print from the *List* view, first switch to it by using the toolbar or home screen, then click *File>Print* from the menu.

❷ **Print all records** When you print a list, you will want to see all the records, not just one, so in the *Print* drop-down menu choose the *Records Being Browsed* option. Now click *Properties*.

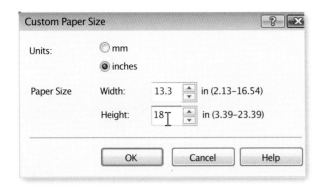

③ Change the page size Using the *Page Setup* tab in the *Properties* dialog, choose a *Custom Page Size*, and set the width as 13.3 inches (34 cm) and height as 18 inches (46 cm). Click *OK*, and set the *Orientation* to *Portrait* back in the main *Page Setup* screen.

④ Print Click *OK* to begin printing. If your list doesn't fit on one page, *Our Family Archive* will print enough pages to include all your records.

Landscape or Portrait

The landscape format accommodates 20 lines per page, while the portrait format allows you to print 50 lines per page. It is important that you choose the correct orientation for your prints, so your lists are printed on the fewest number of sheets.

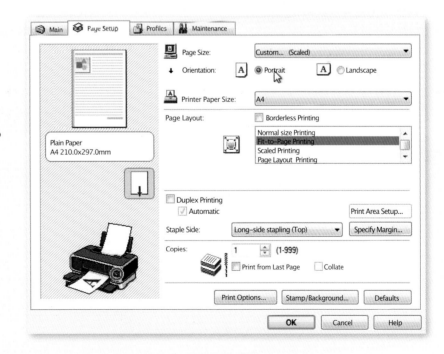

Printing Cards

As demonstrated on the previous pages, you can print from both the *Page* view and the *List* view in *Our Family Archive*. Most printing software also will allow you to print at a reduced size so that you can fit more than one page of the database on a single sheet of paper. This is a great way to make smaller printouts of your archive that you could make into postcard-size books for family members.

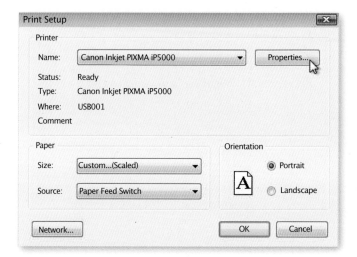

1 **Open print dialog** From any page in the *Page* view, click the *Print* button in the toolbar, then choose *Properties* to open the printer-specific dialog.

2 **Quality settings** Select the paper type that you plan to use. For best results, use branded archival paper made by your printer's manufacturer. Choose the maximum print quality, then click the *Page Setup* tab.

3 **Custom page** In the *Page Size* drop-down menu, choose *Custom* (see page 101), then enter the dimensions of the virtual page again (9.6 x 13.3 inches / 24 x 34 mm).

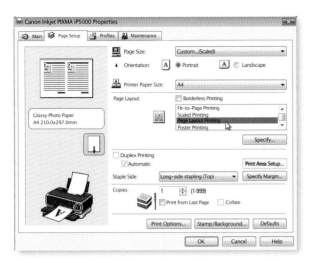

4 Multipage layout From the *Page Layout* menu select the *Page Layout Printing* option.

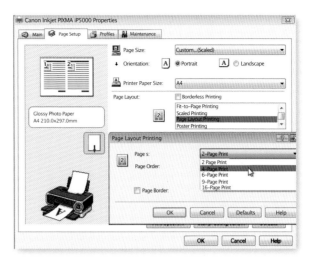

5 Cards to a page Specify how many cards you want to appear on a sheet. Choosing four creates postcard-size prints on a Letter or A4 sheet of paper.

6 Layout You can now decide the order the cards will appear on the page. A Western-style left-to-right sequence is a logical choice.

7 Page and format Finally, check that the page orientation is landscape and that the *Printer Paper Size* is the same as the paper in your printer. Click *OK*, and your printer will print four pages from the archive on a single piece of paper. You can either keep these on a single sheet or cut them up to make a small book of your archive.

Working with Digital Media

Using a computer to archive your family's history allows you to do much more than simply catalog data. With a computer, you can take full advantage of the wealth of information that can be stored digitally. This chapter explores the possibilities (and risks) of digital media of all kinds, but especially those you'll be using for your archive.

In addition to an overview of the equipment you'll need to import pictures, the chapter provides detailed instructions for scanning photos and documents and converting them into digital files. It also includes a section on taking your own pictures with a digital camera and storing them for posterity alongside the other images you've imported from prints.

Why Does Everything Need to Be Digitized?

Everything seems to be digital these days. Not that many years ago, cameras used film, video and audio were stored on magnetic tape, and music could be found on vinyl discs. (Remember records?) Now there are digital formats for each of these media—not to mention the Internet, which, of course, is made up entirely of digital documents we call web pages.

Reasons for Digital Technology

Why has digital technology been so enthusiastically adopted across the board? First and foremost, digitized data does not degrade over time. That doesn't mean you can scratch a compact disc (CD) without risking losing the information on it, but the information itself does not change with the passage of time. Magnetic tapes wear out eventually, even if they're stored and looked after properly, and photographic paper and chemicals are prone to fading. If a CD or other digital information storage medium is handled with a reasonable amount of care, the data files will remain exactly the same.

Second, digital files can be duplicated exactly without any deterioration in quality. The classic example of duplication problems in analog (nondigital) media is the audible hiss on an audio cassette. If you use a dubbing machine to make a duplicate tape, then make another duplicate from that duplicate, the hiss will be louder and the quality is further removed from that of the original. Similarly, if you use a photocopier to duplicate a photograph, the copy won't have the same detail as the original and, just like the tape, a copy of the copy results in lower-quality prints. Digital files, however, can be copied exactly, making it possible to keep a high-quality original while sharing a duplicate with someone else, or simply keeping a second copy as a backup in case the original is lost.

A third advantage of digital files is that they can be easily transferred between computers, and they can be stored much more conveniently than nondigital information, using CD-ROMs, DVD-ROMs, and USB sticks that take up less space.

Your Digital Family Archive

Because your family archive is based in your computer, any information included in the archive will have to be digital as well. Compiling the archive will give you the opportunity to digitize some of your old photos and preserve them electronically. (See pages 116–119).

All of the other information you add to your archive will be in digital form, too, which means that you will have a copy of it for safekeeping. The archive also lets you print out the digital pages stored in the database, with the same quality each time you print and with no need to retrieve—and risk damaging—original prints or documents.

Sharing Files

Once you have converted your pictures, videos, and music files to a digital format you can do a wide range of things with them—from printing your photographs on a home printer, to recording your videos onto a DVD that you can play on a traditional DVD player through your television.

Digital files can be printed as many times as you like at the same quality.

Digital files can be stored or transported using physical media, such as USB sticks.

Most files can be shared between computers of different types.

Digital files can be duplicated identically or converted so they will work on other formats, such as a traditional DVD player.

Modern mobile phones will allow you to store and view files, especially pictures and videos, on the move.

Digital files can easily be sent to and from computers over a network, wireless network, or the Internet.

Types of Digital Files

Digital files come in many formats that are capable of storing information in different ways. Most file types are not relevant to your family archive, because the only files you'll be adding to the database are picture files and there are just four types you need to know about.

TIFF

An acronym for "Tagged Image File Format," this is a lossless format that stores the image exactly as it was scanned or taken. This is important in the professional environment, where TIFFs are most commonly used, because image quality is preserved all the way to the press. At home the large size of TIFF files makes them less practical.

GIF

Usually pronounced "jif," the Graphics Interchange Format can only store a maximum of 256 different colors, which means that it isn't really well-suited for pictures, which normally require millions of shades. Along with JPEG, however, GIF is one of the most common formats on the Internet because the files can be very compact and, therefore download very quickly. If you see a grainy-looking picture on a website, you will find that it is a GIF, saved this way to accelerate download times despite the visible quality loss. It is no longer a sensible format for photos.

PDF

PDF, short for Portable Document Format, is more like a web page or a word-processor document than a photo file. A PDF captures all of the elements of a document (text, graphics, layout, fonts) in an electronic image that is faithful to the original and that can be viewed, sent, and shared with others across computer platforms. For example, you can share the file with someone who may not have the program that created the original document or whose computer or operating system is different from yours. To open and read PDF files, you need Adobe Acrobat Reader, a free download from Adobe, the company that developed the format.

If a PDF is created directly from the computer program used to generate the original document, it's a very efficient way of preserving and sharing the document. The PDF stores the text separately from the pictures, and the pictures—which take up more storage space—may not fill the whole page. However, if you create a PDF from a scanned document or photo, even if that scan is of a text-based document, then the PDF is likely to treat the whole page as an image that loses the advantage of the format unless you use an Optical Character Recognition program (see pages 134–135).

JPEG

Pronounced "jay-peg," this is the most common type of digital image file, and it is almost universally the default option of digital cameras. JPEG stands for Joint Photographic Experts Group (the name of the group that created the format standard), so as you might expect, these files are best suited to photos rather than fine graphics. That's because the photos are reduced by a data compression method known as "lossy compression," which uses special mathematical formulas to eliminate a certain amount of image detail to reduce the overall file size. Therefore you can fit more pictures onto a memory card or your computer, and downloading them is less time-consuming.

The JPEG format also allows you to specify the degree of detail loss. Most digital cameras offer quality settings such as fine, normal, and low on JPEG mode. At the fine setting, it is unlikely that you'll be able to see the difference between the JPEG and an uncompressed file. However, at the low setting, strange patterns called artifacts start to appear around sharp edges, and textured areas can start to lose their detail. *Our Family Archive* can accept JPEG files directly.

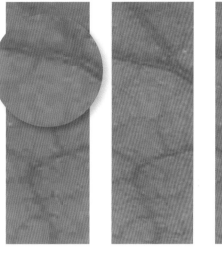
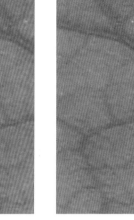

Low   Normal   Fine

Fine

Low

Digital Artifacts

While it is hard to see any flaws in the "Fine" image, the "Low" example has numerous artifacts, which become easier to see around areas of fine detail.

Types of Photographs

Over the years there has been a wide range of photographic technologies. Before you can convert a photo to a digital image, it is very helpful to know the original. This page looks at the most common formats.

In the short time that digital cameras have been on the market, a bewildering variety of digital memory cards have come and—in a few cases—already gone. Even if your format has already slipped into digital history, you will still be able to connect your camera to your computer and copy the pictures from the card to the hard drive using the cable that came with the camera. Failing that, most photo labs can accept a variety of digital media. Film, however, is another story.

Film Formats

Early pioneers of photography experimented by exposing numerous chemicals to light and, until digital technology, the changes were in different kinds of photographic chemicals and media. In the latter half of the 1800s, gelatin plates, then roll film became popular. Just like digital cameras today, there has always been a variety of photographic media, which included 35 mm—the dominant format when digital came along—but it was not the only one. Identifying the format of your pictures is important, because modern labs may only be able to process a few of the older formats.

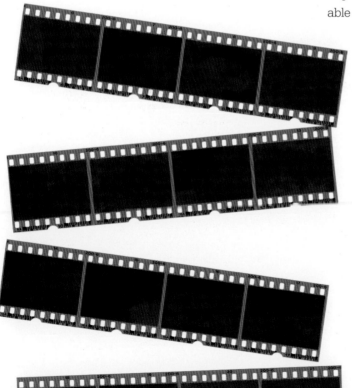

35 mm film negatives
A processing lab usually returns prints with the original film, which is developed into negatives. The color of your negatives will look strange to the eye, but they can be used to make additional prints whenever needed.

Plate camera
Older cameras did not use rolls of film. Instead, glass plates coated with a photographic emulsion, or large, single sheets of film, were used.

As well as the formats illustrated here, there were many other original formats, including Kodak's 1982 disc film system, which had a rotating disc enclosed within a plastic cartridge, with room for 15 exposures around the edge. And before the disc, Kodak produced 110 "Instamatic" cartridges that included two spools so there was no need to rewind the film.

Positive and Negative

Film is usually processed by a lab and returned with any prints, as negatives. Black-and-white negatives reverse the tones, so light areas of the image appear dark and vice versa. Color negatives add a number of other shades into the equation, but it is still the opposite of what you would expect. The alternative—positives or slide film—appear with the correct colors, and this includes prints and transparencies.

Cartridge film
This is an unexposed 35 mm film cartridge, indicated by the a small amount of film poking out. When this is inserted into the camera, the film feeds to another spool as it is exposed. Once the film is fully exposed, it is wound back into the light-proof cartridge before the camera door is opened.

Film Spools
Not all film came in cartridges. The larger formats are spooled from one (unexposed) reel to another (exposed) reel inside the camera.

APS cartridge
APS film is never exposed to the elements, except at the lab and in the camera. There is a four-step marker at the bottom of the cartridge that indicates whether the film inside is new, partially exposed, fully exposed, or developed.

Home Scanners

A scanner is possibly one of the most useful accessories you can attach to your computer. You'll need a scanner to add pictures to your family archive, but you also can use it to make digital copies of documents or to scan photos for other purposes.

Some printers have built-in scanners that enable you to make copies without having to turn on your computer. But to add images to your family archive, you not only have to scan them, you also have to save them as digital files, and for that, your computer has to be turned on, connected to the scanner, and set up to use it.

A scanner and a computer usually exchange information via a cable linking their respective USB (Universal Serial Bus) or FireWire ports. Some scanners are powered via the computer connection; others also have to be plugged into an outlet to work.

To use a new scanner, you first have to install the software drivers and scanning software that came with it onto your computer so it can communicate with the scanner. You only need to do this once; from then on, you'll be able to activate your scanner from any graphics programs on your computer, such as Windows Photo Gallery and Mac OS X's Image Capture, which are provided for free with the respective operating systems.

An advantage of this setup is that any additional graphics program you add to your computer also will be able to access your scanner's driver. Whichever program activates the driver will be the one to which the image is imported from the scanner. If you want to repair an image, for example, you could launch a more sophisticated program such as Photoshop Elements, which also allows direct access to the scanner's driver.

Once you've completed a scan, you will be able to save the image in a standard digital format using your computer's *Save* command. It is this file that you will be able to import into your family archive.

Tip://interpolated resolution

One of the biggest pitfalls in choosing a scanner is the manufacturers' claims about resolution. The higher the scanner's optical resolution, the more detail it can record, so the better quality your image will be.

However, the software supplied with many scanners can increase the resolution by scaling beyond the scanners maximum physical capability, then filling in the blanks using a digital algorithm. This can only ever be the computer's estimation, so the results are rarely very useful, much like the maximum digital zoom setting on a digital camera.

Film Scanner

If you are an avid photographer, it might be worth investing in a dedicated film scanner. This type of scanner features a high-resolution image sensor designed to extract maximum detail from the small area of a transparency so the resulting scan can be scaled up in size.

Flatbed Scanner

A standard flatbed scanner works by moving a bright light and a sensor past an image. The light and sensor are housed beneath a glass platen—similar to the document area of an office photocopier—and the image is placed facedown on the platen. A simple, entry-level flatbed scanner is relatively inexpensive, can make great scans, and is probably all you need for your family archive project.

Flatbed Scanner with Film Scanning

Flatbed scanners that can scan slides and negatives, as well as prints and documents, tend to be thicker than standard, print-only models because their lids need to be thick enough to form a light-proof seal around a slide holder. In other respects, however, the two types of flatbed scanners are similar in design and function.

Scanning Services

If you don't have a scanner, or if you have a standard flatbed scanner but would like to scan slides or negatives, you always can turn to a scanning service. The technicians at a scanning service will be able to generate digital image files from your film negatives, prints, or slides, and deliver them to you on a CD-ROM for copying onto your computer. Even if you have a scanner that can handle transparencies, you may need a scanning service anyway because of the many different and unfamiliar film formats that you're likely to come across as you dig into your family's past.

When you contact any scanning service, the first thing to find out is whether they'll be able to work with your material. Make sure, too, that you don't ask for (or agree to) more than you need. The drum scanning offered by professional bureaus may be an unnecessary expense. With resolutions of more than 10,000 ppi (pixels per inch), drum scans are very high quality—the greater the resolution, the more detailed the scan—but that level of resolution is way above the average 100–200 ppi of most computer monitors, or even the 300 ppi generally required for printing. A scan of a 35 mm transparency made by a regular film scanner might have a resolution of 4,000–7,000 ppi, not quite as high as a drum scan, but still more than good enough to use in your family archive or to make an 8.5 x 11 inch (22 x 28 cm) print. For more on digital image resolution and display, see page 126.

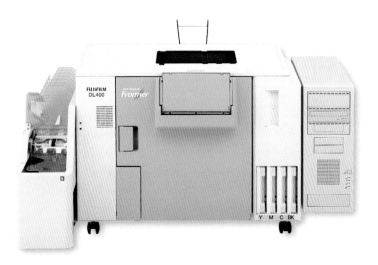

Minilab
Many professional photo labs, especially those offering services such as one-hour photo development, use minilabs to process 35-mm film into prints. Newer models also include scanning devices that enable labs to offer digital image files on CD-ROMs, too.

Something else to consider when arranging for the scanning of your precious prints—especially if they are originals that you cannot replace—is how you will transport them. When you discover them stored in the loft, a forgotten cupboard, or the garage, it's likely that they have been undisturbed for a long time. As soon as you begin to move them, their integrity is at threat. All paper—including photographic paper—gets increasingly brittle as it ages, and changes in temperature and humidity will also affect the paper.

Your first task is removing the photo from wherever you discovered it—it may have become stuck to the glass in a picture frame, or the plastic film in its display album, for example. It's important you don't apply too much pressure trying to remove it in case you damage the photograph, and sometimes it may be better to leave it and try to re-photograph or scan it in the frame or album.

Once you've removed the pictures to scan, they should be placed between two sheets of hard board to safeguard from light (which will cause fading), and from creasing.

Tip://finding a scanning service

If you're trying to scan old photographic prints or transparencies, your local photo lab will probably have the equipment and expertise required, especially if you're dealing with an uncommon film format. A copy shop will be able to scan from prints, documents, or slides, but it might be less familiar with old film types.

Drum Scanner
High-end professional scanning services use drum scanners capable of resolutions of more than 10,000 ppi. At that level of resolution, you can scan a 35-mm slide, transfer the scan to a printer, and create a full-quality (300 ppi) print as large as 45 x 30 inches (114 x 76 cm).

Scanning Pictures

If you have a scanner connected to your computer, the process of scanning your own pictures at home is relatively straightforward. The instructions in this section are for scanning printed photographs, as opposed to transparencies, such as slides or negatives. Scanning transparencies is somewhat more involved, as you'll see in the first box below. Remember, too, that there are a number of scanner manufacturers, and sometimes they provide additional or different solutions, which will be included in the instructions.

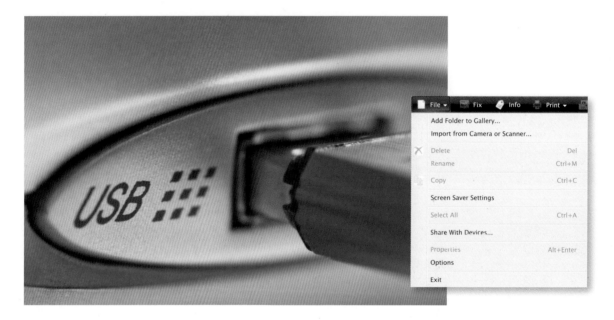

1 **Check connections** Before you start, be sure that your scanner is switched on and connected to your computer, and, if necessary, to the electricity supply. If you need to disconnect another device to free up an outlet, make sure the device is not in use.

2 **Launch the graphics program** Launch the graphics program of your choice—for example, the Windows Image Library program. From the menu select the *Import* or *Import from Scanner* option, and choose your scanner from the list of devices. If you don't see the scanner, check to make sure you have properly installed it.

Tip://scanning transparencies

To scan a slide or a negative, you'll probably have to place the transparency in an accessory holder and choose the *Slide* or *Transparency* mode in your scanner's software. Consult the manufacturer's instructions for more details.

3 **Prepare the scanner** Once your scanner's software window appears on the screen, open the scanner's lid and, if necessary, use a lint-free cloth to wipe off any dirt or dust from the glass platen.

4 **Insert the document** Place your photograph facedown on the platen, and line it up against two of the glass platen's edges—the optimum corner is usually marked with an arrow, and different page sizes are indicated along the platen's frame. When you are happy with the photo's position, gently close the lid.

5 **Preview the scan** Click the *Preview* option. The scanner will perform a quick, low-resolution scan of the entire document area. The result will be shown in the dialog box on your screen.

New Scan

Scanner: EPSON Perfection 4870   Change...

Profile: Photo [Default]

Source: Flatbed

Paper size:

Color Format: Color

File type: JPG [Snapfire Image]

Resolution (DPI):   300

Brightness: ──────○────── 0

Contrast: ──────○────── 0

☐ Preview or scan images as seperate files

See how to scan a picture   Preview   Scan   Cancel

→

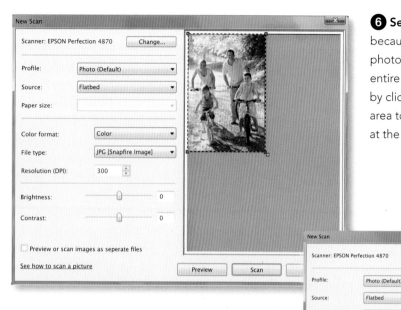

6 Select the scan area The preview is useful because it allows you to select the area of the photograph you want scanned—either the entire photo or a specific detail. Select the area by clicking in the top left-hand corner of the area to be scanned and releasing the mouse at the bottom right.

7 Adjust the resolution Once you've marked the scan area, you also need to adjust the resolution of the final output. If you want a scan that will allow you to make a good-quality print at the original size, 300 ppi is a good choice. However, if the picture is very small and you would like it to appear larger on the computer screen, scan it at higher resolution. For example, 600 ppi would double the image size.

8 Pick the color setting Even if the photo you are scanning is black and white, select the high-resolution color setting—either *Photo*, *Full Color*, or *16.8 million colors*, depending on your brand of scanner. This setting will provide the most detail.

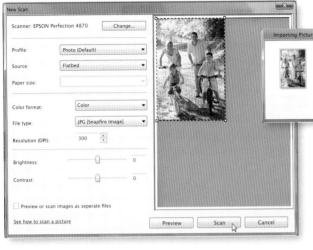

9 **Scan the picture** Click the *Scan* button, and wait for the scanner to perform its duties. There may be a brief delay while the scanner light warms up, and then the scan head will start its slow move across the image. Because it sends more information back to the computer, the actual scan takes longer than the preview scan.

10 **Add a label** Your software might label the image automatically, but you can also add keywords, such as names, separated by commas. This makes searching for pictures easier later.

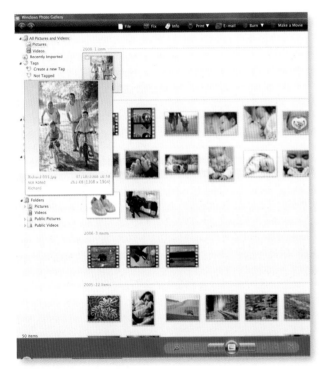

11 **Check the result** Once the scan is completed, you will be returned to the graphic program that you were working with. Use that program to see the result, and check that the quality is what you hoped for. in Windows Photo Library you can just hover the mouse pointer over the thumbnail.

Tip://resolution and quality

If you choose to increase the resolution of your scan in order to get a larger digital image (see step 7, page 122), bear in mind that you are limited by your scanner's maximum optical resolution. Scanner software frequently offers very high resolutions, such as 6,000 ppi, but these are almost always interpolated by the computer software (see Sharpening Digital Files, page 128). The maximum optical resolution is the highest true recording the scanner can make. That doesn't mean you cannot use the interpolation to scale up the image, but similar to the digital zoom on a camera, the results may not be very sharp.

Taking Pictures for the Archive

A family archive is not just about your ancestors; it is also about your living relatives. Chances are that you already have a good supply of photos of your relatives, but there's always room for more. Also, a photo taken for archival purposes is different from a family snapshot, which is often shot with a messy background, uneven lighting, or other people present. It will only take a few minutes of your time to shoot more formal portraits of your relatives, which can show them off to their best advantage.

Setting Up

In addition to high-end cameras, a professional photographer uses a great deal of expensive equipment to light the model and support an appropriate background. Fortunately, it's possible for a nonprofessional to take excellent photos without having to invest in fancy equipment.

When picking a background for your model, use something plain; good choices include a painted wall or plain drapes. Drapes with a very small pattern will also work, but try to avoid large or bright patterns that will draw attention away from your subject.

To light your model it is best to use a diffused light source that won't create harsh shadows. Professional photographers place their lights in large "softboxes" with a translucent side, or they use special umbrellas to reflect their lights. A cheaper alternative is to shoot your photograph near a window in good sunlight. If that isn't possible, you also can place some tissue or Scotch tape over your camera's flash to soften the light.

Teacher portrait
A blackboard makes a great background because it highlights the subject's profession and it is also relatively plain.

Angle of Light

The angle of the light on your subject's face is important. If it comes from directly behind the camera, it can leave the face looking flat and unnatural—often a problem with camera-mounted flashes. The best solution is to set the light at a 45-degree angle to your subject, so the person's features are textured, but no area is left too dark.

Shooting Angle

If possible, ask your subject to move their head slightly to the left or right while keeping their eyes on you or the lens. Position the camera so that the lens is level with your subject's eyes, then shoot a few frames. One advantage of digital photography is that you can shoot plenty of shots and delete the ones you don't want.

Side lighting
In this case, the light from the camera's left side is stronger than the right—thanks to daylight coming in through a net curtain.

Tip://no rules

Remember that there are no strict rules to your photography, and you can include any digital images you like in your family archive database. Instead of taking a formal portrait against a plain background, why not try photographing a relative with a favorite object in their hand or at one of their favorite places?

Close crop
A very close crop on faces reveals a lot of character. It is a good idea to stand at a distance and use the zoom or the subject's features will appear warped.

Scaling Digital Files

Digital images are made up of tiny bits of information called *pixels*. A digital image often consists of millions of pixels, and the greater the number of pixels making up an image, the more detailed the image will be. This is why camera manufacturers promote the number of megapixels (millions of pixels) their cameras can capture in a single photo. Once an image is captured, however, another measure becomes important, too—the image *resolution* expressed in pixels per inch (ppi). It is this combination of pixel count and pixel density that tells a computer how to display and print a picture.

One thing to remember about ppi is that it is inversely proportional to image size. An image's ppi is a fixed number of pixels per square inch. Decreasing the ppi spreads those pixels out over a larger area, thereby increasing image size—and vice versa. For example, a 1-inch-square picture at 300 ppi becomes a 2-inch-square picture when its resolution is lowered to 150 ppi.

Viewing Images

While resolution is important for printing images, it is less crucial for viewing images on a computer screen or working with programs such as *Our Family Archive*. Most software programs look only at an image's pixel count (not ppi) and translate image pixels to screen pixels, usually in a one-to-one ratio, or at 100 percent. An image on a computer screen is viewed at 100 percent if one pixel in the image is displayed as one pixel on-screen.

Most programs allow you to temporarily alter the zoom on an image while you are working. This doesn't affect the number of pixels in the image, but zooming out will fit the whole picture on-screen at once, while zooming in lets you see small details.

Scaling and Resizing

Some programs also allow you to scale, or resize, an image. This is a more permanent alteration that does affect pixel count. Reducing an image to 50 percent results in a significant loss of detail. If you save the reduced image and then scale it up 200 percent (back to its original size), you won't see the same level of detail as you did in the original image. That's because the computer had to discard data in order to render the image with only a quarter the number of pixels (half width and half height) it originally had; when you scaled back up, the computer had only the reduced number of pixels to work with.

Our Family Archive works at standard computer resolutions, which means that images from a digital camera or a scanner will usually be much larger than what you actually need. Digital cameras and scanners can capture as many as eight-to-ten megapixels, whereas an average computer monitor can display approximately one megapixel. It's a good idea to keep a copy of the original high-resolution scan and save a smaller, less space-hungry version under a different file name for actual use in *Our Family Archive* and other programs.

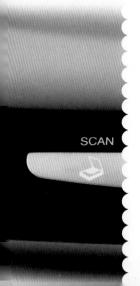

Resolution: 40 ppi,
95 x 95 pixels

Scaling settings:
Resample: On
PPI: 40
Dimensions: Untouched

Image Scaling

This diagram illustrates the principles of image scaling in an exaggerated way. To make the pixels clearly visible, the pictures have been reproduced at resolutions of 40 ppi and 80 ppi. All computer screens vary, but the arbitrarily chosen technically correct resolution for on-screen work is either 72 ppi or 96 ppi. Upward of 200 ppi will make a good photo print, although 300 ppi is the minimum generally used by professionals.

Resolution: 160 ppi,
190 x 190 pixels

Resolution: 80 ppi,
190 x 190 pixels

Scaling settings:
Resample: On
PPI: 160

Resolution: 160 ppi,
380 x 380 pixels

Sharpening Digital Files

Despite what you often see in crime dramas, it's not possible to bring an out-of-focus picture into sharp detail. If the camera didn't capture information when the photo was taken, there's no way a computer can reconstruct something from nothing. There are, however, several ways to manipulate a digital picture—either from a camera or a scanner—to make it seem sharper. These techniques are applied to the individual pixels of an image, and they need to be used only after you've brought the image to its final output or viewing size. At that stage, however, you'll find that it's often possible to work minor miracles.

By their very nature, most digital files—especially those from digital cameras—will look slightly soft. That's because when an image is captured, stored, resized, or otherwise digitally manipulated, it undergoes a process called interpolation, which adds new pixels to the image based on an analysis of its existing pixels. Among other things, interpolation allows you to make larger prints without decreasing resolution (*see page 126*), but the process does result in some loss of image quality each time it occurs.

Image Sharpening

The sharpening tool of a computer graphics program acts as an antidote to digital interpolation. In a nutshell the tool identifies areas in an image where there is contrast—usually the edges of shapes—and exaggerates it slightly, making the overall picture look sharper.

Different programs vary in their names for their sharpening tools. The traditional one, which has

Smart Sharpen Tool
The *Amount* slider adjusts the strength of the sharpening effect, while the *Radius* slider tells the computer how far out from an edge (in pixels) it should increase contrast. Make sure the view is set to 100 percent to see how the effect is applied to individual pixels; any other size will be subject to some kind of distorting interpolation, making it less reliable.

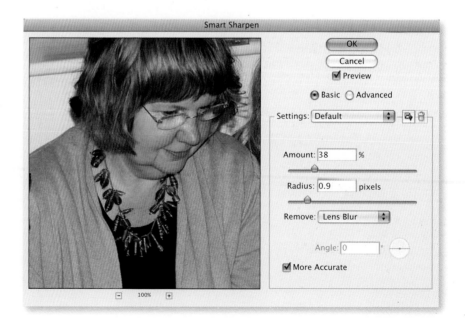

Here is the same image before sharpening and with different amounts of sharpening applied to it.

Original

been used by professionals for years, is *Unsharp Mask*. The name sounds less strange when you realize that what the tool does is hide, or mask, "unsharp" areas. Newer tools, like *Smart Sharpen*, use more sophisticated techniques to identify the areas that need the most attention, but the principles are still the same. Both of these tools exist in Adobe Photoshop and Photoshop Elements.

If you want your pictures to look better in *Our Family Archive,* follow the directions on page 126 to scale them to their final size. Save the scaled file under a new name in order to preserve the original high-resolution version, then launch the sharpen filter. Adjust the strength of the effect until it looks right and resave the image with a new name.

Sharpened

Tip://soft images

In most digital cameras the image sensor consists of an array of tiny photosites, each corresponding to a pixel in the final image. The photosites are filtered to allow only one color of light—red, green, or blue—to penetrate each photosite cavity. The filters are arranged in a pattern, but each pixel in the final, full-color digital image includes red, green, and blue information. To supply the two missing color channels in each pixel, the camera analyzes the colors in surrounding photosites to arrive at the final color for each pixel. This process of approximating missing colors results in the softer edges of many digital images.

Too Sharp

Scanning Documents

Making a digital copy of a document is very similar to scanning a photograph. There also are tools you can use to make an old document look like new in its digital form, if that's what you prefer. Many people, however, consider that the yellowing of the paper and a few marks and tears give an old document, such as an ancestor's birth certificate, a certain amount of character. There is no reason to eliminate signs of age on a document if you don't want to—the choice is entirely yours.

Handling old documents requires care, since the paper is usually not as strong as photographic paper. Documents are particularly vulnerable near the edges or along creases and folds, so take special care when unfolding them. If the paper has been badly damaged or is more than 200 years old, consult an expert.

Before touching the paper, wash and dry your hands, then make an effort to slow your movements so that when you actually touch the paper, you'll be gentle and deliberate about it. Be especially careful if the paper seems unusually stiff; that means it is more likely to be brittle and easily damaged.

Given the difference between paper composition and content, scaning documents requires a slightly different approach. Here's a step-by-step guide to getting the best results when scanning documents, although it's important to note that some of the steps are optional.

1 Launch your image-editing program, and begin the scanning process as described on page 120. If your scanner has a *Special Document* mode, it's worth experimenting with, but for this tutorial, *Photo* mode is the better choice. It gives you more control and usually captures a greater level of detail. The *Document* mode is better suited to newer paper and blacker inks than you're likely to find in aging documents.

2 Place your document facedown on the scanner's glass platen. If the sheet is in good condition, you'll be able to line it up against the edge of the platen by gently sliding it in place. If it is heavily misshapen, leave a little space between the edges of the sheet and the platen's frame. Try to position your page so that the text runs parallel to one of the sides of the glass.

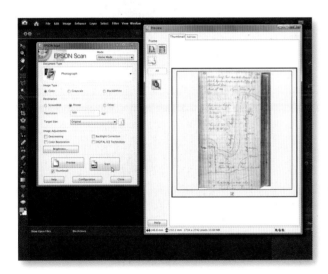

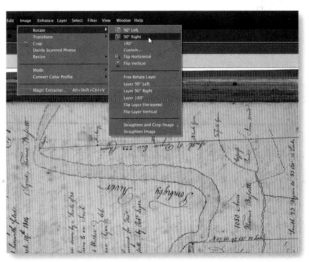

3 Use the *Preview* button to view the scan, and adjust the document as needed. Make a selection that includes the whole document, and scan it at high resolution.

4 When the image appears in your image-editing program, make sure that the text is oriented correctly by rotating the image as needed. In Adobe Photoshop Elements the rotate options are accessed by clicking *Image>Rotate* and choosing from the *90° Right*, *90° Left*, or *180°* options.

→

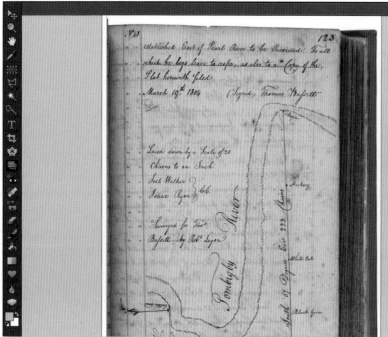

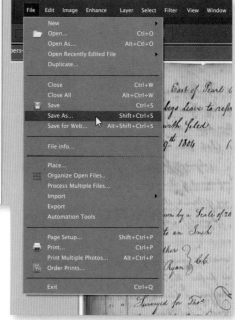

5 If you need to fine-tune the rotation, select the *Straighten* tool from the *Tool Options Bar* and then click at the bottom of a character at one end of a line of text. Drag the mouse, without releasing the button, to beyond the other end of the line of type. When the line is exactly aligned with the bottoms of all the characters in the line of type, release the mouse.

6 If you like the way your document appears at this stage, you can simply save it as a JPEG file ready for inclusion in *Our Family Archive*. If, however, you would like to increase the document's clarity, continue to the next step.

7 Create a new *Levels Adjustment* layer by clicking on the *New Adjustment Layer* button in the *Layers* panel and choosing *Levels*.

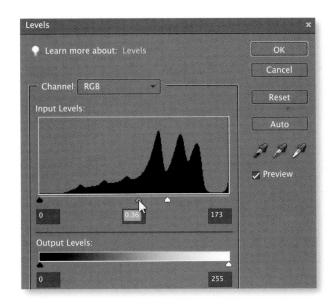

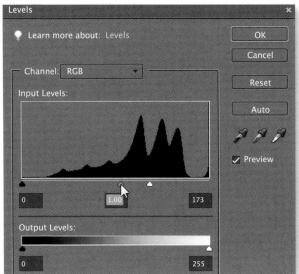

8 In the *Levels* window, you'll see a histogram that will have a clear spike near the right-hand end. This spike represents the paper, which will be a lighter color than the ink. To adjust the document so that the light shades appear completely white, move the highlights slider beneath the histogram from the far right until it's on the opposite side of the spike.

9 This has the effect of making the background white, but you'll also notice that the type has gotten lighter, too, making it difficult to read. To darken the type, click and drag the *Midtones* slider to the right, toward the one you just moved. This tells the computer to darken shades between gray and black, which will include the type. Click *OK* when you are happy with the results.

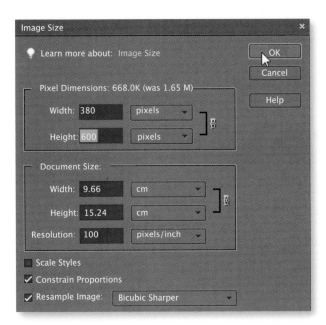

10 Reduce the size of your document to something more practical for *Our Family Archive* using the *Image>Resize>Image Size* dialog. Save it as a JPEG under a new file name. You will now be able to import the picture of the document into your family archive in the same way as any other picture file.

Optical Character Recognition

In the previous sections you learned how to scan a document, save it as a picture file, and import it into the *Our Family Archive* database. Scanning is the usual way to digitize a document, especially if it's a highly visual one, such as a passport with a photo. For longer, text-based documents, however, there is another option: Optical Character Recognition, or OCR. As the name suggests, this is software that enables a computer to read a document and convert it into a digital text file that you can save on your computer.

An electronic text file is considerably smaller than a scanned image, so it saves a lot of space on your computer. If you decide you would like to store some text documents along with your family archive, OCR is much faster than typing in lengthy text by hand. The technology still has some accuracy issues, and the older and more damaged the document, the less likely it is that any OCR software will be able to read it. Newer and more powerful OCR software can deliver more accurate results, but the most important thing is to make sure that the best possible copy of the document is getting to the program.

Acquiring the Document

One way to import a document into an OCR program is to photograph it with a high-resolution digital camera. Set up the camera so that it points down directly at the piece of paper. Light the document evenly by pointing a lamp at it from either end of the sheet, and be sure to focus accurately.

You will get the best results, however, with a scanner, even a modestly priced one. It is likely that your OCR program will have a *Scan* button, allowing you to begin the process directly. If it doesn't, scan the document as described on pages 130–133. For the highest-quality image, save the scan as a TIFF file, before opening it in the OCR program.

Digital Conversion

Once the document is in the OCR program, you may need to indicate which block of text is to be scanned—this is usually a simple process of drawing a box around the text by clicking and dragging with the mouse. After that, all you have to do is wait a few moments for the software to work its magic, and then you'll be able to save the document as a text file and open it in your word-processing program.

The best way to find out if OCR software is useful for you is to try it out. To give you an idea, the next page shows some examples of how the software performs on two different documents.

Tip://getting OCR software

If you have a scanner, it is worth checking the CDs supplied with it—you might find a free OCR program. If you don't have a scanner and you're a Windows user, you can download free OCR software from *www.freeocr.net*. Mac users, however, will have to consider a commercial package, such as Readiris Pro. For more details, check the online resources page at the back of this book.

Older Document

This old telegram is a good example of a document that is difficult for OCR software to process. The weight of the letters varies, but the software has the most trouble in the places where scratches and pen marks have been added. It simply cannot understand them.

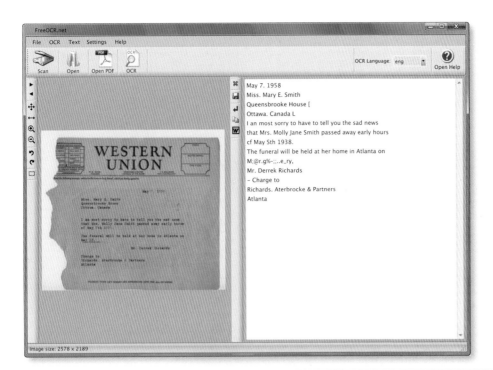

FreeOCR.net

File OCR Text Settings Help

Scan   Open   Open PDF   OCR   OCR Language: eng   Open Help

```
May 7. 1958
Miss. Mary E. Smith
Queensbrooke House [
Ottawa. Canada L
I an most sorry to have to tell you the sad news
that Mrs. Molly Jane Smith passed away early hours
cf May Sth 1938.
The funeral will be held at her home in Atlanta on
M;@r.g%-;;..e_ry,
Mr. Derrek Richards
- Charge to
Richards. Aterbrocke & Partners
Atlanta
```

Image size: 2578 x 2189

Newer Document

This much more recent solicitor's letter is better preserved, without marks, and is printed to a better standard with a modern printer. The software has much less trouble identifying the characters, although this OCR program has still lost the formatting.

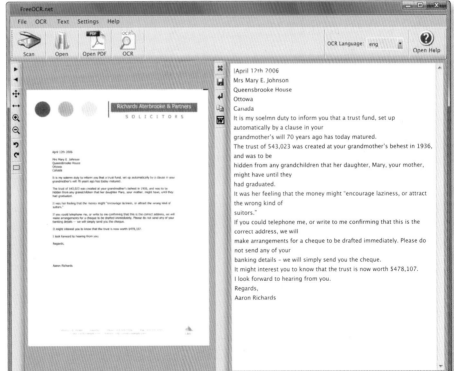

FreeOCR.net

File OCR Text Settings Help

Scan   Open   Open PDF   OCR   OCR Language: eng   Open Help

```
|April 12th 2006
Mrs Mary E. Johnson
Queensbrooke House
Ottowa
Canada
It is my soelmn duty to inform you that a trust fund, set up
automatically by a clause in your
grandmother's will 70 years ago has today matured.
The trust of 543,023 was created at your grandmother's behest in 1936,
and was to be
hidden from any grandchildren that her daughter, Mary, your mother,
might have until they
had graduated.
It was her feeling that the money might "encourage laziness, or attract
the wrong kind of
suitors."
If you could telephone me, or write to me confirming that this is the
correct address, we will
make arrangements for a cheque to be drafted immediately. Please do
not send any of your
banking details – we will simply send you the cheque.
It might interest you to know that the trust is now worth $478,107.
I look forward to hearing from you.
Regards,
Aaron Richards
```

Image size: 2578 x 2189

Digital
Restoration

The great thing about getting your images onto the computer is that you can work on them digitally without risking damaging the original. With your old photographs this gives you the opportunity of repairing any damage to restore the picture, adding special effects, or coloring a black-and-white original.

This chapter shows you how to do all of these things, which gives you the potential to bring your family history to life in a whole new way. Whether you want to subtly tone a picture to match your favorite *Our Family Archive* theme, or give an older picture a new lease of life, the following pages will show you how.

Restoring Damaged Photos

One of the best things about preparing your family archive is that you get to find and enjoy as many captivating old photos as possible. You can add up to six photos to each person's record, so there's plenty of chance to show off all the best ones.

The problem is that photographs taken before the digital era don't age well. Once an image is stored digitally the details remain the same unless the image file is edited or saved in a different file format, but paper prints can easily be damaged by moisture, scratches, and tears, or simply fade over time.

The solution is to use a computer graphics program to restore the image to its former glory. If you haven't already done so, the first step is to get the picture onto the computer using a scanner. After that you can edit it in your favorite graphics program.

2 Setting the view Select the *Zoom* tool from the *Toolbox* and choose the 1:1 mode from the *Tool Options* bar. This scales the on-screen image to 100 percent, which means one pixel in the picture file is represented as one pixel on your monitor, giving the most accurate possible preview as you work.

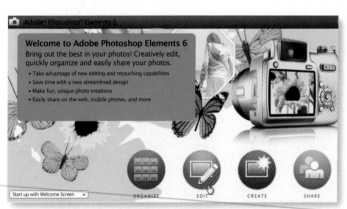

1 Image editing software A damaged photo needs more sophisticated software than a basic browser, so launch a program like Adobe Photoshop Elements, and choose the *Editor* mode. Open the scan of your damaged photo using the *File>Open* menu.

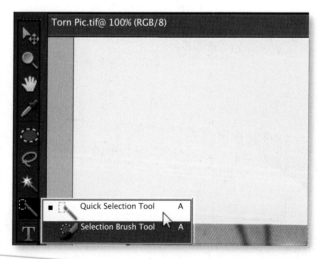

3 Selection tools Select the *Quick Selection* tool from the *Toolbox*. Sometimes this tool is hidden behind the *Selection Brush* tool, depending on which you used most recently. In that case, click and hold the mouse down on the icon and choose the *Quick Selection* tool from the pop-up menu.

4 **Highlighting the torn piece** Click and drag the mouse across the torn area to select it. An outline will appear around the area you have selected, and as you move the mouse, more will be added to the selection.

5 **Default colors** Make sure that the *Foreground Color* is set to white by switching the default colors. Press D, or click on the *Foreground/Background* color boxes.

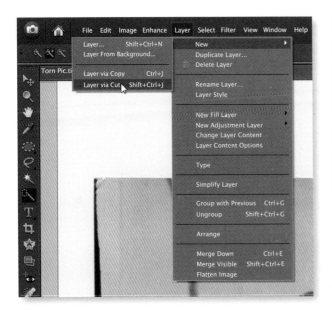

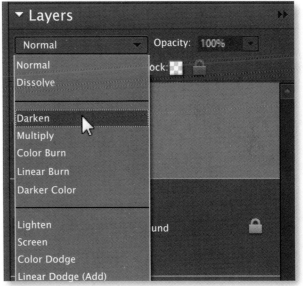

6 **Splitting layers** When you have selected the entire torn area, click *Layer>New>Layer via Cut* in the menu. This moves the selected area onto a new layer that you can move around and line up with the rest of the picture.

7 **Blending modes** In the *Layers* panel you will see a new layer. Click on it to select it, then set the *Blending Mode* to *Darken* by clicking on the word *Normal* and choosing *Darken* from the drop-down menu.

→

8 **Moving the torn piece** Adjust your view so you can see the whole damaged area on the main part of the picture, then select the *Move* tool. Make sure that the selected layer in the *Layers* panel is Layer 1 (the newly created copy), then click and drag the torn-off section and line it up as close to the tear is possible. You can use the cursor keys to make single-pixel movements for extra accuracy.

9 **Cropping damaged edges** Using the *Zoom* tool as you did in step 2, click the *Fit Screen* button, before choosing the *Crop* tool. Click and drag across the picture area, moving the mouse from the top left to the bottom right of the area you want to keep. This is a useful way to eliminate the rough edges, and it will save you time repairing the picture.

10 **Merging layers** Before you can make repairs to all the blemishes, you need to flatten the image into a single layer. Do this by clicking *Layer>Flatten Image* in the top menu.

11 **Choosing the right tool to repair damage** To repair blemishes and small scratches to your picture, select the *Spot Healing Brush* tool. This tool, like other brush tools in Photoshop, will apply its effect to the area beneath the mouse pointer. To change the size of the brush use the [or] (square bracket) keys.

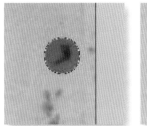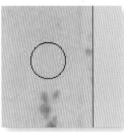

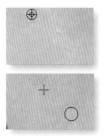

⑫ Painting over damage Adjust the brush size so it is slightly larger than the area you would like to clean up, then click on the spot, or paint along a scratch. Repeat this process over all the blemishes that are in plain areas of the picture. The *Spot Healing Brush* will try to intelligently work out what the texture and color of the damaged area needs to be and correct it.

⑬ Manual tools Sometimes the *Spot Healing Brush* tool can get confused, leaving results like the one shown. If this happens, press Ctrl/Apple+Z to undo and switch to the regular *Healing Brush*. This tool allows you to Alt+Click on a source area before painting over your blemish. The source should be an area of the same texture as your blemish. If this tool fails, undo again and try the *Clone Stamp* tool, which works in the same way but copies color and texture exactly.

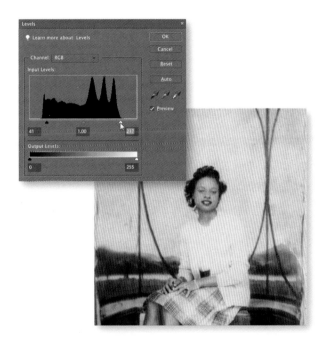

⑭ Correcting color tones with levels To adjust the picture's color balance, create a new *Levels* layer, and click the *Auto* button. This will automatically correct color and contrast, though you can still tweak the overall effect by sliding the arrows beneath the histogram.

Restoring Faded Photos

No matter how or when they were shot and processed, printed photographs tend to fade over time. Once you've scanned a faded print, however, it's possible to restore the image to its former glory, thanks to the magic of image-enhancing software. And better yet, the process is largely automatic. You can fine-tune the results afterward, too.

The following step-by-step sequence will show you how to restore the faded colors of an old photograph and how to save the restored image for inclusion in the *Our Family Archive* database.

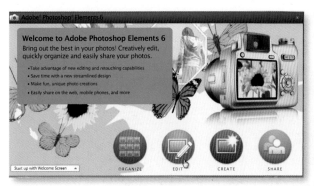

1 **Edit mode** Launch Photoshop Elements, and select the *Edit* mode.

2 **Scan the faded image** To scan directly into Photoshop, make sure your scanner is connected and then click *File>Import>[name of your scanner]*. If the picture has already been scanned and is stored on your computer, open the file using the *File>Open* menu option. If you have already stored the picture in the *Our Family Archive* browser, locate it from there and double-click on it.

3 **Adjustment layers** The most effective option for correcting fades is *Levels*, because it can address each of the three colors that make up a digital picture (red, green, and blue). Create a new *Levels* layer by clicking the *New Adjustment Layer* icon at the bottom of the *Layers* panel and then click *Levels*.

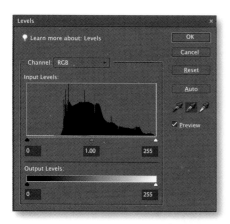

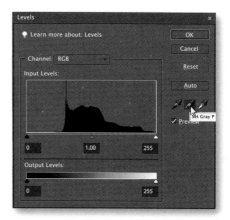

4 Levels adjustment In the *Levels* window you will see a histogram (see *Histogram and Levels* box, below) and three eyedropper icons—black, white, and gray. Click on the middle (gray) eyedropper.

5 Adjusting the tone Select a neutral tone somewhere in the image, preferably an area that should be gray or, failing that, a part of the image that should be black or white. Click on it, and you'll notice the picture change in tone, hopefully to one that looks right. If it doesn't look quite right, try clicking on another neutral area. Click *OK* when you're happy with the result.

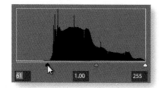

Tips://histograms and levels

• A histogram is a type of bar chart with peaks that show the relative tones (the lightness or darkness) of your picture. The histogram is a handy tool for diagnosing exposure problems, but in a *Levels* adjustment layer it has an additional purpose: You can use the sliders beneath the histogram to adjust the look of the picture.

• When you move the left-hand *Shadows* slider toward the right, the darker elements of the picture are set to black and all the other tones are shifted along to keep the result natural-looking. Similarly, the right-hand *Highlights* slider will brighten the lighter areas. The central midtones adjustment can be used to lighten or darken the picture overall.

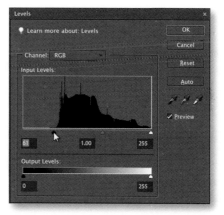

6 Adjusting the contrast You also can use the *Levels* tool to fix the contrast. Drag the black slider located at the left of the histogram toward the right until the slider is beneath the first significant peak. This will darken the shadow areas. Next drag the white slider located at the right end of the histogram toward the left to brighten the lightest parts of the picture.

→

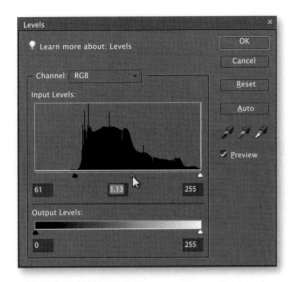

7 **Midtone adjustment** To adjust the overall brightness, you need to use the midtone slider. For a slightly lighter image drag the central (gray) slider to the left—or to the right for a darker result overall. This picture was lightened slightly.

8 **Rich colors** If the color is not strong enough for you, create a *Hue/Saturation* layer by clicking on the *New Adjustment Layer* icon at the bottom of the *Layers* panel and choosing *Hue/Saturation*.

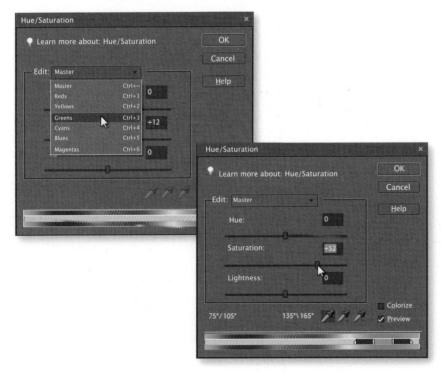

9 **Overall saturation** Drag the *Saturation* slider to the right to increase the strength of all the colors. If you don't want to adjust all of the colors (or "hues"), click on the drop-down *Edit* menu at the top of the window and pick the colors you want to strengthen.

⑩ Save As...
When you have
finished adjusting
the color, click
File>Save As... and
choose *JPEG* from
the *File Type* menu.

Tips:// alternatives to Photoshop Elements

- When it comes to color restoration, Photoshop Elements is not the only program you can use. Photo-editing programs, such as Paint Shop Pro or GiMP (GNU Image Manipulation Program), also include a *Levels* feature. Windows Photo Gallery and Apple's iPhoto, however, do not.

- You also might want to take a look at one of the newest versions of Photoshop, called Photoshop Express (shown left). This is an online image-editing program that means the program is stored on Adobe's website, not your computer. You can use the program for free by visiting *https://www.photoshop.com/express/*. All you need to do is choose the picture on your computer that you want to use, and you can edit it in your Internet browser with Photoshop Express. When you've finished editing it, you can save the result back onto your computer.

Tinting Your Photos

Tinting is an effect you might use just for the fun of it or to give all the pictures on a page layout the same look. The classic tint choice is sepia—a color that aging prints tend toward anyway—but there are plenty of other possibilities.

Not only does tinting have more than one use, it can be done by more than one program, including, conveniently, the *Photo Gallery* tool built into most versions of Windows Vista. The only downside is that the changes made will affect the file they're made to, so it's wise to make a copy of your color original before getting started.

2 *Fix* **mode** To enter an *Editing* mode, click *Fix* in the toolbar. A number of options, including *Adjust Color*, will appear to the right of the picture. Click on this to select it and open additional options.

1 **Locate the image** Locate the picture that you'd like to tint in the *Windows Photo Gallery*. As you hover your mouse pointer over the pictures in the catalog, a larger preview will appear. Click on your chosen picture to highlight it, or double-click on it to see a large view.

3 **Eliminating color** Before you can make a tinted image, you need to remove the existing color. Slide the *Saturation* slider to the far left to remove all color.

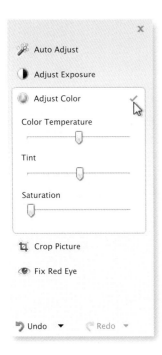

4 Confirming your change To confirm that you're happy with the new black-and-white picture, click on the checkmark at the top of the *Adjust Color* options group.

5 Back and forth Once you've eliminated the color, the other controls won't be very useful. You need to go back to the Gallery view by clicking *Back to Gallery*, at which point the color original is replaced with the black-and-white version.

6 Open again Click on the newly converted image in the Browser screen, just as you did in Step 1, and once again open it in *Fix* mode.

7 Adjust *Color Temperature* The *Fix* mode will operate as if it had never seen the file before, so now you can adjust the color by tweaking the *Adjust Color* sliders. Move the *Color Temperature* slider to the right for a yellow sepialike tone.

Tinting to Match the Themes

If you're tinting your pictures as described on the previous page, using a sepia tone is by no means compulsory. If you chose to experiment a little with the *Temperature* and *Tint* sliders, then you'll already know that there are other color and shade options available to you.

Since you've got the tools, why not tint your photos to match the color of the theme you chose for the archive page they appear in? Here are the basic steps, as well as the color combinations to match all 12 themes.

❶ Create a black-and-white original Follow the steps on pages 146–147 until you get to step 6. This will leave you with a black-and-white image and the *Adjust Color* tools open.

To make the color change, adjust the three sliders using the examples in the box to guide you. The tone of the image needs to reflect the theme you've chosen for that entry in the archive.

❷ Create a new archive As you create or edit a record in *Our Family Archive*, make sure you select the same theme by clicking on it (see pages 70–73).

❸ Insert the edited photo Add the picture using the method described on page 73, step 12. Select the newly edited photo. This will replace the original picture in the location in which it was stored on your computer.

❹ Click *Preview* To see your picture in its matching background, click *Preview* in the data entry page, and you'll be taken to the final page layout.

Settings

These are the settings to copy (see step 2) to match a tinted photograph to each of the themes in the program.

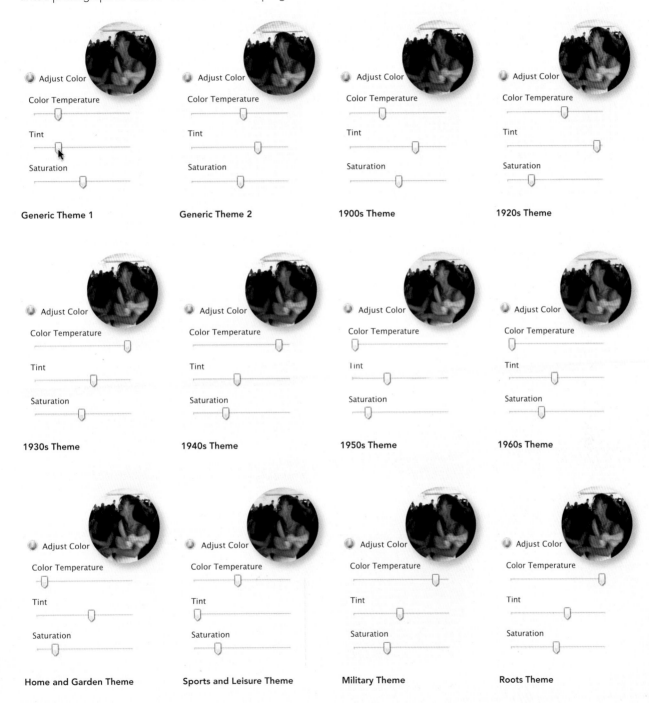

Generic Theme 1

Generic Theme 2

1900s Theme

1920s Theme

1930s Theme

1940s Theme

1950s Theme

1960s Theme

Home and Garden Theme

Sports and Leisure Theme

Military Theme

Roots Theme

Coloring Black-and-White Prints

One thing you'll certainly come across as you look through old family pictures is numerous black-and-white prints. Monochrome photographs are synonymous with the past, since modern color film has only been available since the mid-thirties.

While there is a certain charm, not to mention historical accuracy, to black-and-white prints, there's also a good argument to be made for livening them up with color. We see life in color, and the addition of a more realistic palette can make the past come alive in a whole new way.

❶ **Preparation** To make sure you can color an image, you need to tell Photoshop that it's a color image, not a black-and-white one. To do this, open the picture and choose *Image>Mode>RGB Color*. You are now ready to add color.

❷ **Add a coloring layer** Create a new empty layer by clicking on the *New Layer* icon at the top of the *Layers* panel. This is the layer you will be coloring. Adding color to an empty layer means that you can make changes to the color without affecting the picture itself.

③ Selecting an area to color Sometimes it's easy to paint using the brush tool, but at other times you can make a selection to mask off an area so that you don't go over the edges. To make a selection, choose the *Quick Selection* tool, choose *Select All Layers* in the *Tool Options* bar, then click and drag the tool roughly across the target area.

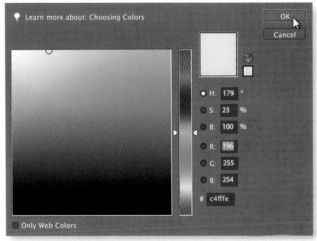

④ Coloring the selected area To color in a selected area, click on the *Foreground Color*—the colored square at the bottom of the toolbox—and pick the shade that you think (or know) that area needs to be. Switch to the *Brush* tool.

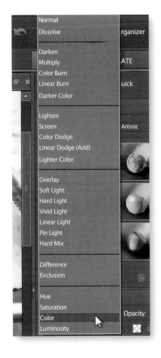

⑤ *Color* mode Before you begin painting, click the *Mode* drop-down in the *Layers* panel and set the blending mode to *Color*. This allows you to add color to the empty layer, but the detail from the picture on the layer below will still show through.

→

6 Painting Click the mouse button and start to paint over the highlighted area to add color to the new layer. The area will quickly start to look as if it were shot in color.

Tip://relative strength

If you remember to keep using new layers for new areas of color, you can use the opacity slider to adjust each area's strength. Click on the layer you want to alter, then click on the *Opacity* slider and move it with the mouse. You will see instant feedback on screen, and if you don't like the result, just move it back to 100 percent.

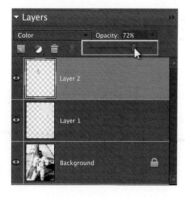

7 Unselected areas To work on the rest of the picture, deselect the area by clicking Ctrl+D. You can now choose to make a new selection or to brush by hand. If you choose to brush by hand, zoom in to at least 100 percent using the *Zoom* tool.

Tip://
automatic recoloring

If the method shown here seems a little arduous or is asking too much of your mouse hand, there are alternatives that make coloring easier. One option is a software program called Recolored. You can download a demo version to try it for yourself, or purchase it at *www.recolored.com*.

8 Controlling the brush When painting by hand, choose a brush of medium hardness by clicking the *Brush* drop-down in the *Tool Options* bar and setting the hardness to 50 percent. You can increase and decrease the size of the brush using the square bracket keys.

9 Use more layers Continue to color different parts of the picture. It's wise to use a new layer for each color, so that you can edit all the colored layers separately. Changes might include going back to a layer and using the *Eraser* tool if you find you've brushed over the edge a little or adjusting the color using *Hue/Saturation*.

Taking Your History Online

In what seems like no time at all, the Internet has become perhaps *the* essential communications and publishing tool, making it easier than ever to share your thoughts and your pictures with friends and relatives, whether they are on the other side of town or the other side of the globe.

The main Internet technology is the World Wide Web, which dominates Internet traffic so much that people often refer to it erroneously as the Internet. In reality, the Web is just one of the information resources and services—e-mail is another—that are carried on the Internet.

In this chapter you'll find an overview of the Internet and how it works, as well as a guide to creating a simple website on which you can share your family's history with the world.

How the Internet Works

The Internet has revolutionized the way the world works, communicates, learns, and plays. But what, exactly, is the Internet? This is a complex topic, but in a nutshell, the Internet is a group of computer networks that are interconnected and able to exchange data with one another using standardized methods of communication known as protocols. Among the information services and resources carried via the Internet are e-mail, online chat, file transfer and sharing, and the system of interlinked hypertext documents, images, and other resources known as the World Wide Web.

Internet Protocols

Think of protocols as the language computers use to communicate with one another. The main set of communications protocols used for the Internet is TCP/IP (Transmission Control Protocol/Internet Protocol). The protocol you may be most familiar with is Hypertext Transmission Protocol, better known by its acronym, http, which appears (followed by a colon and two slashes) before Web addresses. When you type a web address into your Web browser and press *Return* on your computer, a request is sent to that address by your computer. The request travels though gateway computers known as "domain name servers," which act like sorting offices, making sure the request gets to the right place—namely, the computer that stores, or hosts, the requested Web page. When it receives your request, the host computer immediately sends you the Web page it has stored at that address.

Another Internet protocol you may come across is File Transfer Protocol or FTP. Instead of being used to send and respond to Web-page requests, FTP allows you to connect with another computer so that you can send files to it and retrieve files from it over the Internet. It is the most common way of putting Web pages on the Internet.

Servers

A Web server is any computer that can understand http requests and respond by transmitting a Web page. In theory this could be your computer, but in practice that's usually not feasible. For one thing, your computer would have to be on at all times to function as a Web server dealing with requests from other Internet users to access your Web pages. For this, and other reasons, most individuals (and many companies) use an Internet Service Provider (ISP) to host their Web pages.

ISPs use many different technologies to enable their customers to connect to the Internet, including telephone dial-up, DSL (Digital Subscriber Line), cable modem, fiber to premises, and wireless broadband. When you sign up with an ISP, you'll receive its software package, as well as a user name and password that will enable you to log on to the Internet and browse the Web. Many ISPs also offer storage space on their dedicated Web servers so you can upload files that will then be available to the world as your Web pages.

Accessing a Web Page

As this diagram shows, your computer is connected to the Internet via a service provider, such as a phone or cable company. The ISP's server has a permanent connection to the Internet, through which it relays your Web page request to the appropriate host computer.

The red line is the route your request for a page takes, the green line represents the journey back, and the blue line is the route taken by someone else's request to view your Web page, which is stored on your ISP's server.

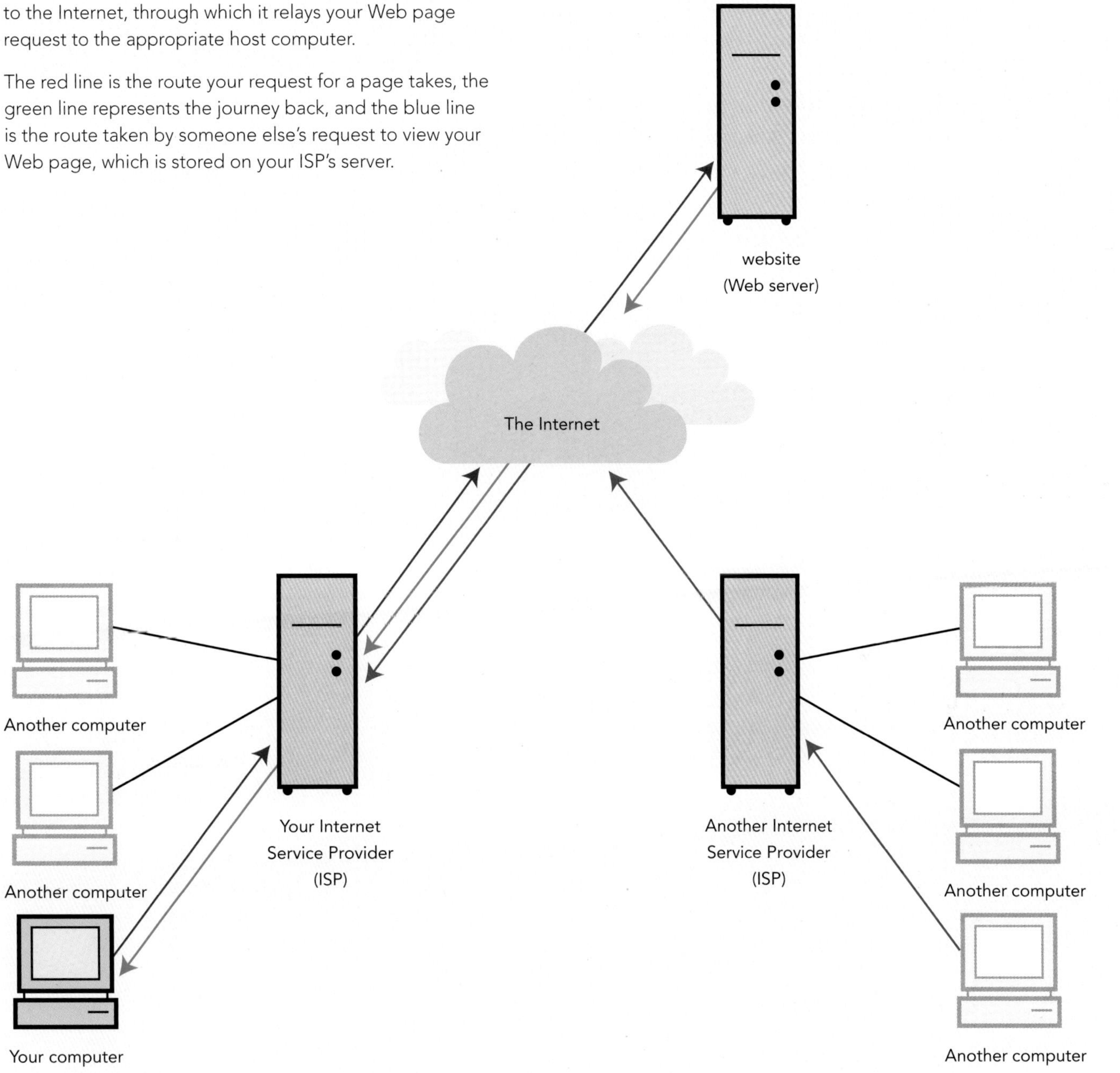

website
(Web server)

The Internet

Another computer

Another computer

Another computer

Your Internet
Service Provider
(ISP)

Your computer

Another Internet
Service Provider
(ISP)

Another computer

Another computer

Another computer

Securing Server Space

If you're not a corporation, it's impractical for you to run your own Web server. It is much cheaper to rent server space from one of the many companies that offer this service. Your Internet service provider's access package also may include a few megabytes of Web storage space, which is more than enough for most personal websites. Once you've acquired server space, you need to copy your files to it. The usual way to upload files to the Internet is via FTP (see pages 156–157). Conveniently, Windows makes copying files to an FTP site as easy as moving files around your own computer. (For the Apple Mac alternative, see the box below.)

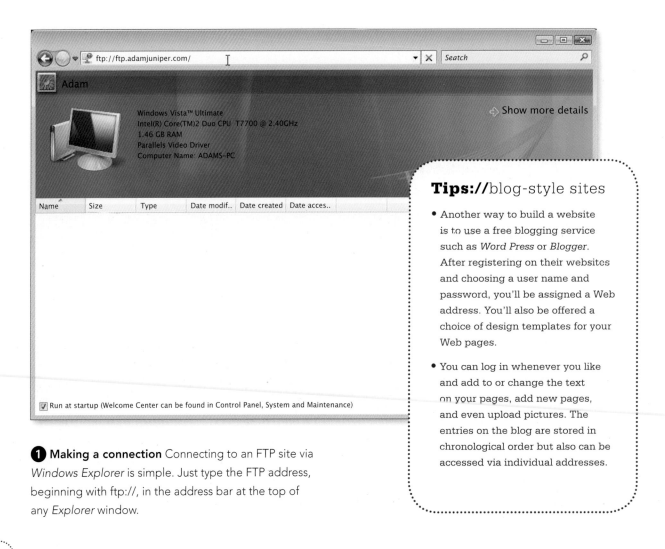

❶ Making a connection Connecting to an FTP site via *Windows Explorer* is simple. Just type the FTP address, beginning with ftp://, in the address bar at the top of any *Explorer* window.

Tips://blog-style sites

- Another way to build a website is to use a free blogging service such as *Word Press* or *Blogger*. After registering on their websites and choosing a user name and password, you'll be assigned a Web address. You'll also be offered a choice of design templates for your Web pages.

- You can log in whenever you like and add to or change the text on your pages, add new pages, and even upload pictures. The entries on the blog are stored in chronological order but also can be accessed via individual addresses.

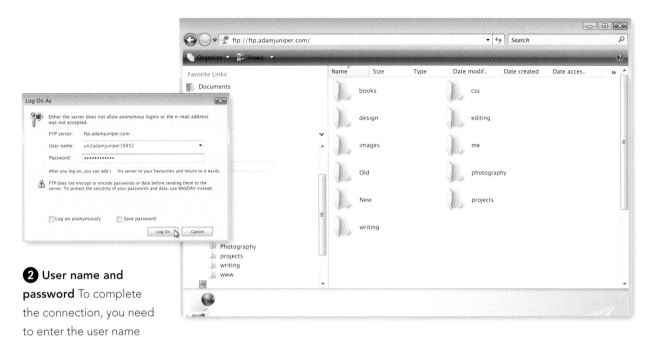

2 **User name and password** To complete the connection, you need to enter the user name and the password you established with your ISP or Web host.

3 **Explore and upload** The *Explorer* window now displays the contents of your Web space. You can upload pages and pictures to this space by dragging them from another *Explorer* window.

Tip://the Mac solution: iWeb or CyberDuck

All Macs are supplied with a program called iWeb, which allows you to build your own Web pages and, if you subscribe to Apple's *MobileMe* service, to upload your pages directly onto the Internet.

Another option is a program called *CyberDuck*, an FTP tool for Macintosh computers that you can download for free at *http://cyberduck.ch/*

Simplified Site Building

What if you don't want to go through the hassle of posting your own Web pages on the Internet but still want to create a distinctive site? Fortunately, Google and other Internet companies have created systems that let you make Web pages and build up your site quickly and easily through your Web browser.

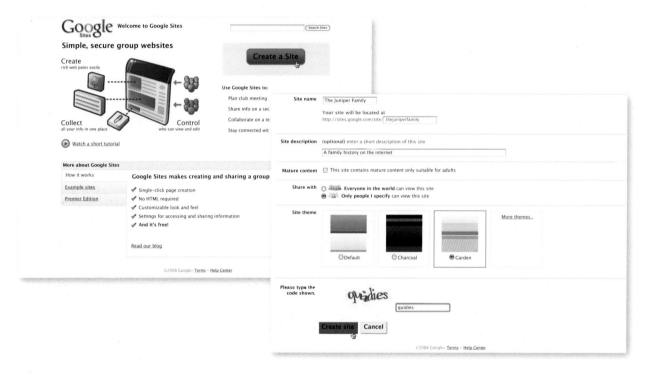

❶ Google Sites Launch your Web browser (Internet Explorer, Mozilla Firefox, or Safari, for example), and go to *http://sites.google.com*. If you already have a gmail account (an e-mail account through Google) you can use the same password, otherwise you'll have to register for one, which takes a few moments.

❷ Create a new site Click the *Create New Site* button on the Google Sites page, and follow the instructions on-screen. Select a style, or design theme, for your site from the options offered, enter the access code shown at the bottom of the screen, and click *Create Site*.

❸ Edit page In the page that appears, click the *Edit Page* button. Dotted outlines will create two rectangular areas. Click inside either box to type in text. To begin, change the word "Home" to the name of the relative you want to feature on his page.

4 **Adding links** Highlight the name you've just typed, and click *Link* in the toolbar. This will call up a window that offers you several options. Choose *Create New Page* from the bottom of the dialog, and name your new page after the same relative.

5 **Copying details** If you open the *Our Family Archive* program while you are still running Internet Explorer, you can copy and paste text from the archive to the page you are creating. Click on the *Edit* button in *Our Family Archive*,

highlight the text you want to copy, and press Ctrl+C. Click back to Internet Explorer, and click in the main text area of that relative's page, then press Ctrl+V to place the text.

6 **Adding pictures** You can create more pages in the same way, but without pictures they will be a little dull. Luckily, it's as easy to add images to your new site as it is to add text. Click *Insert* on the toolbar, and choose Image. In the pop-up window that appears, click *Choose File* and click *OK*.

7 **Sharing your pages** Continue building your site. If you don't want to make the site visible to everyone, you can limit its access to just your friends and family. To do that, click *Site Settings* at the top right of the screen, and type the e-mail addresses of the friends and family members you want to share the site with into the *Invite People* box. Choose *As Viewers*, and then click *Invite These People*. You'll be able to add your own message to invite people to look at your site.

Preparing Files for the Internet

Knowing how to upload a Web page to the Internet is one thing, but you also need to know how to create the page in the first place. A Web page is a document that is written in HTML (short for HyperText Markup Language) and then translated and displayed by Web browsers. In addition to the HTML text file, Web pages usually include instructions on how the page should look, as well as links to images that are to appear on the page. A Web page also may contain hypertext links that take you to other Web pages, so to create a Web page, you'll need to generate several different files.

HTML Text Files

Commonly used word-processor programs, such as Microsoft Word, make it easy to create Web pages. To see if your word processor can save a document as a Web page, open a new document and then click on the *File* menu. If you don't see an obvious Web page option (*Save as Web Page*, for example), click the *Save…*or the *Export* options in the *File* menu and look for an HTML or .htm option. If there is one, type whatever you like in the text document, then save it as a Web page using the Web option. The front or home page of a website is usually named *index.html*.

JPEG Image Files

The JPEG format used by most digital cameras is also the most widely used graphic format on the Internet. Save your images in this file format before using them on your Web page.

Links

In order for you to place images in your document, your Web program has to save the links to the pictures' locations. Images aren't automatically copied into the Web page—the program just remembers which file it should display—so you need to remember that both the images and the Web page need to be uploaded to your Web space, not just the page itself.

> **Tip://**blog-style sites
>
> When adding links to images or other web pages, you do not need to type out their full address in the form *http://www.yoursite.com/page.html*. Instead you can use a relative link, so if you are linking to a page or picture saved in the same folder as the page you are editing, you only need to type "link.html" or "link.jpg."

Creating a Web Page
To save a document as a Web page in Word, select *File>Save as Web Page.*

Before You Upload
This folder shows you how to organize your website files before uploading them. Collect your pages and images in a single folder on your computer, and then upload the entire folder to your Web space.

Resources

This chapter features a convenient troubleshooting guide as well as an extensive glossary of computing terms, so there's always somewhere to turn if you find yourself getting stuck. You'll also find some useful advice on copying the data from your computer onto another one if you upgrade your computer system.

Troubleshooting

No matter how much you try to avoid it, things go wrong from time to time. This page presents some of the most common problems you may encounter along with some solutions to them. While every effort has been made to cover all possible problems, *Our Family Archive* is a computer program, so some problems might only exist when used on future computer systems. That's why there is also a website you can check for the latest advice if you aren't able to find the answer you need here.

When I put the disc into my computer nothing happens

When you insert the CD into your computer, it will take several seconds before anything happens. This is because disk drives take a few moments to spin up to speed. If you use a Macintosh, a disc icon will appear on the desktop but a window will not appear. This can be quite easy to miss, especially if you have a cluttered desktop, or have windows obscuring the desktop, so be sure to check again.

If you are using a Windows computer, the disc uses the *AutoPlay* feature to launch a special window to begin the install process. Some users choose to disable the *AutoPlay* feature, which means you'll have to locate the files yourself, using the method described on page 54.

If the computer is not recognizing the disc at all, try ejecting it and reinserting it. Inspect the surface of the disc for damage and, if necessary, wipe it off using a lint-free cloth. Always wipe CDs gently, from the center outward rather than in a circular motion.

Can I use the program directly from the CD?

The *Our Family Archive* program is supplied on a prerecorded disc, so it's important that you install it on your computer's hard drive before you begin. Although you can run the program from the CD, you cannot save any new information, so anything you add would be lost when you quit the program.

To copy the program onto your computer, follow the instructions for your computer system: Windows PC pages 54-55, Apple Macintosh pages 56-57. This copies files from the CD to the computer's hard drive so it can be run without the CD.

I have installed the program, but I cannot find *Our Family Archive* on my Windows computer

Our Family Archive will be added to the *Start* menu alongside your other programs. You can launch it by clicking the *Start* button. If you cannot see it straight away, click on *All Programs*. The program is stored within a directory next to a tool to remove the program, if necessary.

I cannot find *Our Family Archive* on my Macintosh computer

On an Apple Macintosh, your programs are all installed in the *Applications* folder. After following the instructions on page 56, you will find a folder called *Family Archive* within your *Applications* folder. Inside that is the *Our Family Archive* program. Double-click on it to launch it.

I would like to make *Our Family Archive* easily accessible by using the *dock* on my Macintosh computer

Launch the *Our Family Archive* program from the *Applications* folder as described above, then press Ctrl and click on the program's icon in the *dock*. Choose *Keep In Dock* from the pop-up menu. Now, even when the program is not running, you will see *Our Family Archive* in the *dock*, and you can launch it with a single click.

How do I remove *Our Family Archive* from my Windows computer

If you want to uninstall *Our Family Archive* from your PC, you can by clicking *Start* and going to the *Our Family Archive* folder in the *Start* menu. You will find an automatic uninstaller program that will delete the program and any information that you added to it.

How do I remove *Our Family Archive* from my Macintosh computer

If you want to uninstall *Our Family Archive* from your Mac, you can by dragging the *Family Archive* folder from the *Applications* folder to the *trash*. Be aware that this also will delete all the data that you added into the program, because this is stored alongside the program in the file named Data.USR.

→

I have bought a new Mac computer and I want to copy my files from a PC and continue working on them

Unfortunately it's not possible to transfer the information from a Windows PC to a Mac, or vice versa. However if you bought a new Windows PC and you want to move the data from your old one, you can. The process is a little involved, and requires you to know the administrator password for both computers, but the steps are simple.

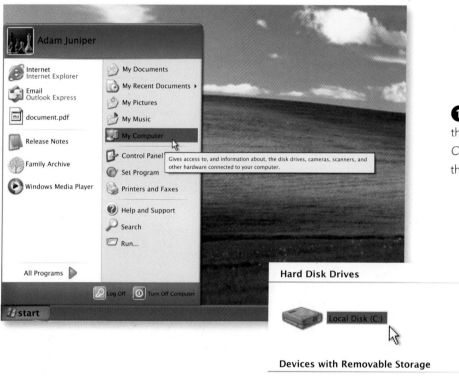

1 **On the old computer** Click on the *Start* button, and choose the *My Computer* option to see a folder of the computer's contents.

2 **In the *My Computer* window** Double-click on the Local disc (C:/) drive icon. This is where *Our Family Archive* is located if you followed the automatic options during installation. If you changed the options, you will need to look wherever you chose to install the application.

3 **Open the *Program Files* folder** This is where all the components of *Our Family Archive*—as well as the other programs on your computer—are kept. You may get a warning message reminding you not to make changes to the files. Proceed anyway, but remember not to alter or delete any files.

4 **The *Program Files* folder** Inside this folder you will find the *Our Family Archive* folder. Open it.

5 **Locate the Data.USR file** This file contains all of the elements of the *Our Family Archive* that you can change—all the words and pictures that you have added—in a single file.

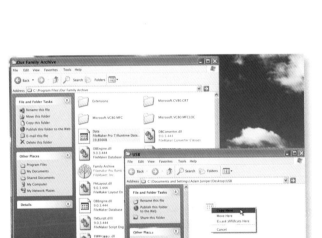

6 **Copy the file** You now need to copy the Data.USR file from its current location to a new one. You can use a variety of media, or a network connection if you have one, but one of the most practical devices is a USB memory stick. While holding the Ctrl button, click and drag the Data.USR file from the *Program Files* folder to your storage location, then choose *Copy Here* from the pop-up menu.

7 **On the new computer** Install the *Our Family Archive* program on your new computer, but do not launch it.

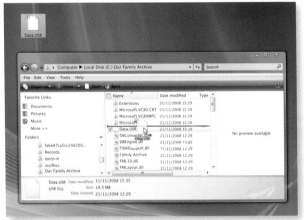

8 **Windows XP or Windows Vista** If your new computer has Windows XP, open the *Our Family Archive* folder in the *Program Files* folder as youy did before, and replace the Data.USR file on your computer with the one you copied onto your memory stick.

If your new computer uses Windows Vista, then you will find the program folder in the C:/ drive, called *Our Family Archive*, without needing to look inside the *Program Files* folder.

Glossary

Blu-ray Disc

A new standard of computer disc for High Definition video. Blu-ray discs are similar in appearance to CDs and DVDs, but they have a much higher storage capacity. A recordable version is available.

Broadband

A collective term for different methods of high-speed Internet access. These include leased lines, cable, or DSL solutions. Broadband is recommended if you need to download large files from the Internet such as movies or transfer images to an online lab because of its speed.

Burning

In computer terminology the verb "to burn" refers to the act of recording information to a CD, DVD, or Blu-ray Disc (known collectively as "optical media").

Button

A graphic or icon on your screen that you can "press" by clicking on it with your mouse.

Cine film

Sometimes called Ciné, the word literally means "moving." It refers to the home-movie formats that existed before video-based systems. These are 8 mm, 9.5 mm, 16 mm, and Super 8.

Checkbox

A box that you can click on to select a property that is usually named next to the checkbox. When the checkbox is selected, a check mark will appear in the box. Clicking on it again will deselect—or uncheck—the box.

Codec (EnCOder-DECoder)

A common word for the software that helps your computer unlock an audio or video file format. For example, if you want to play a video file encoded with MP4, you will need the MP4 codec installed on your computer. This is normally built into the operating system on your computer.

CD-R and CD-RW

These are writable (CD-R) and rewritable (CD-RW) discs based on the CD format (see CD-ROM). Computers can record, or burn, data onto these discs.

CD-ROM (Compact Disc Read Only Memory)

A disc that uses the same design as an audio CD, but stores computer information and can only be read by computers, not audio CD players.

Data

A computer term to describe any information. You might say, for example, that once you have created a new record for the name and address of one of your friends you have "added data to the name and address fields."

Digital Versatile Disc (DVD)

A high-performance disc format that was originally designed as the Digital Video Disc, but was adopted by computers because of its ability to hold a large amount of computer data. A DVD can store 4.7 GB (single layer) or 9 GB (dual layer).

Directory

A specially named area, or folder, stored on a computer disc. You can place files within a directory.

Exporting

The process of saving a file—or group of files—from an editing or cataloging program. The files can be saved in a common format that is likely to be compatible with another program, such as JPEG or TIFF for images, or MP3 for audio. For example, you might export a photograph from a catalog as a JPEG file so you can import it into the *Our Family Archive* program.

Field

The individual boxes within any of the records in *Our Family Archive* that you use to add information. For example "First Name" is a field, because it only requires you to add one separate piece of information.

Finder

The finder is the component of Mac OS X that allows users of Apple Macintosh computers to navigate the files, folders (also known as directories), and applications stored on the computer, on inserted discs, and on any network connected to the computer.

FireWire

A common name for the IEEE 1394 or i.Link standard conection. This is a common socket on computers and digital devices, which was designed for the reliable high-speed transfer of large amounts of data, such as video, and the control of external devices. It is common on digital camcorders, which can be controlled using stop, play, and wind buttons from the computer.

i.Link

A trade name used to describe the FireWire or IEEE 1394 connection standard.

Importing

The process of moving a file into another program and, if necessary, converting it into a format that is compatible with that program. The term is often applied when you are copying images from your digital camera to an image-cataloging program.

iPhoto

A photo-cataloging and image-editing program supplied with all new Apple Macintosh computers.

iTunes

A free music-cataloging program for both Apple Macintosh or Microsoft Windows computers. This is an ideal tool for keeping track of a music collection.

Joint Photographic Experts Group (JPEG)

This is the most common file format for digital images. If you have a digital camera, it will almost always save files in this format. Its popularity stems from its efficiency in compressing images to fit onto the limited storage space of digital media. It achieves this by discarding some of the details according to settings you choose when you save the file from an image-editing program or in your camera.

Lossy compression

Compression that discards some of the detail in order to create smaller computer files. JPEG picture files and MP3 audio files both use lossy compression.

MPEG (Motion Picture Experts Group)

This is a common form of computer video file, often identified by the file extensions .mpeg or .mpg. Like JPEG, it uses a lossy compression to reduce file sizes, and subsequent versions of the standard MPEG-2 and MPEG-4 (also known as MP4) have continued to dominate computer video.

MPEG-1 Audio Layer 3 (MP3)

Usually known by its abbreviation, MP3 files are the most common way of saving music on computers and portable players. Portable players, such as Apple's iPod, are often known simply as MP3 players.

Network

A network is formed by the connection of two or more computers. Files can then be shared without having to copy them onto external discs.

Photoshop Elements

Photoshop Elements is a digital image-editing program that can be bought separately and installed on your computer. It has a variety of tools for repairing and changing your digital images. There are different versions available for both Apple Macintosh and Microsoft Windows computers. The latter also includes an image-cataloging function, while the Mac version works with iPhoto's catalog.

Pixels Per Inch (PPI)

This refers to the level of detail in a digital image file. It is especially important when you are acquiring the file (for example, scanning it). A typical scan intended to be viewed only on-screen at 96 ppi means that every square inch of a picture would be represented by $96 \times 96 = 9,216$ pixels. A good resolution for digital files is 96 ppi. If you are printing files, 300 ppi is better—but it uses more file space.

Premier Elements

This is a digital video-editing program from Adobe—the same software manufacturer as Photoshop. It has a variety of sophisticated tools, including the ability to edit High Definition video and exporting it to the latest Blu-ray discs.

QuickTime

QuickTime is a common video file format on both Apple Macintosh and Windows computers. A program to play the files, called QuickTime Player, is available for free from Apple (www.apple.com). QuickTime can also play files based on open standards, such as MPEG.

Raw file

High-end digital cameras, especially Single Lens Reflex (SLR) cameras, can save Raw files. These files include all of the original information seen by the image sensor, and all of the information recorded by the camera's onboard measuring devices, but processing is not applied. Instead, the processing is handled by the computer when the file is imported. Therefore, the maximum amount of information is available when images are processed on your computer. The disadvantage is that the processing stage is mandatory, and the software must be aware of your specific camera model to interpret the Raw data.

Record

A record is a single entry in *Our Family Archive*. For example, if you add the details of a relative, you create a single record composed of their name, date, and place of birth, education, occupation, and so on. The individual parts of the record are called fields.

Rip

The process of converting one type of digital file—usually audio or video—to another.

Scanner

A device for converting printed photographs, slides, or negatives into computer files.

Tagged Image File Format (TIFF)

A standard file format for saving image files that is commonly used by professionals because it does not discard any details. This is known as a "lossless" file format, but as there is no compression of the data, the file sizes can be very large.

Universal Serial Bus (USB)

The most common socket for connecting peripheral accessories to a computer. USB and USB 2.0 use the same sockets, automatically switching to the faster speed—or bandwidth—available when both the computer and USB device are USB 2.0 compatible. USB devices include printers, mice, external hard drives, scanners, and more. USB cables can even carry a certain amount of electricity, so some devices don't need an additional power supply.

USB Hub

If you don't have enough USB sockets on your computer, you can connect a hub that allows you to plug more than one device into the same socket.

World Wide Web (Web)

You can look at, or browse, pages that are stored on computers around the world by using a Web browser. These pages, or websites, are the ideal place to find photographs and conduct research if you want to add detail to captions in *Our Family Archive*.

Windows Explorer

Windows Explorer is the part of Microsoft Windows that you use to navigate the files and folders stored on your computer's hard drive and any external media that you have inserted. Explorer also allows you to browse the contents of other computers via a network.

Photo Credits

Alfred Eisenstaedt/Pix Inc./Time Life Pictures/ Getty Images 47; Arthur Schatz//Time Life Pictures/Getty Images 46L; iStock 6, 7BL, 11L, 12, 15TL/TR, 16-18, 18BL, 20L, 21-22, 23TL/BR, 24L/R, 26, 28, 29TR, 30-32, 33TL, 36BR, 37-42, 44L, 45BR, 46BR, 48BR, 50, 61L, 68, 84, 97BL, 99T, 108, 111BR, 114, 115TL/TR/R, 118, 124-125, 127L, 136, 154, 162, 164, 167; John T. Barr/Getty Images 44; Jupiter Images 7T, 8, 11TR, 14, 19T, 33BL, 43, 48L, 52, 120L; Library of Congress 24C, 25, 27, 29L, 33TR/ CR, 34-35, 36BL; Maureen Barratt 23R; Michael Mauney//Time Life Pictures/Getty Images 46C; Philippe Huguen/AFP/Getty Images 45T

Index

Acknowledgments

From Adam—A massive thank you, as ever, to Jules, who put up with me spending days and weeks cultivating my relationship with my laptop at the expense of so much else. Thanks also to Chris and Emily for their well-timed interjections, David for the chapters he wrote, and everyone else who has worked so hard on every detail of every page. Finally, a thanks to my extended family and friends, especially those whose picture appears within these pages.

From David—Thanks to Chris, Adam, and Nick at Ilex for their encouragement and advice during the writing of this book, and to Rosie Barratt for her diligent picture research. I'd also like to particularly thank my wife, Antonia, for her continuing support.

Stmry
24.95

WITHDRAWN